THE SCANDALOUS SCAMPS

THE
SCANDALOUS
SCAMPS

by

HAROLD MEHLING

HENRY HOLT AND COMPANY   New York

The author wishes to thank the magazines which origi-
nally published chapters two, four, nine, and ten in
slightly different form: *Coronet,* for "520% Miller" (first
published in May, 1959); *O.K. for Men,* for "The Blackmail Business of Seducer Cassie" (first published in April,
1959); *Coronet* for "Man with the Green Magic" (first
published in March, 1956); and *Pageant,* for "The Man
with the Atomic Powered Swindle" (first published in
August, 1956).

85657-0119
Printed in the United States of America

For

JANE ELLEN,

who lives near Sing Sing

Foreword

Many of us find it difficult to give the swindler-devil his due. Instead, we berate his victims and claim they were only witless fools anyway. We sigh philosophically and say that people are stuffed with a human frailty known as credulity.

Well, it is true enough that swindlers' victims include a large number of addled ladies and impressionable gentlemen, rarely questioning, endlessly trusting. But among these victims are also a great number of persons whom we habitually regard as hard-headed, shrewd, suspicious of what poses as fact. Can the high incidence of *their* gulling be accounted for by such epithets as foolishness, impressionability, and credulity?

Conveniently, yes. Logically, no. Actually, a successful swindler is a man who skillfully employs great but irresponsible talent, who understands that he must seduce our common sense. He labors day and night, sometimes for years, before making his first overt move. He studies the specialized detail of his field. He strives to look, act, sound, and seem like the character he has elected to become. In the end, he has constructed a proposition that begs for belief.

Too often, we confuse swindlers with less accomplished malefactors. Although we make careful, precise breakdowns of almost everything else in society, when dealing with criminals we simply fill the pot and call it stew.

It is not. If common thieves are stew meat, swindlers are pressed duck. A thief steals money; a swindler exerts a gravitational pull on it. Where a thief is armed with a gun, a swindler is armed with a magician's rod. A thief leaves his victims outraged; a swindler leaves them outmaneuvered.

The question that remains: Why does the swindler swindle? Why does he grow up and suddenly find everyone else going north while he is going south—with the money, if possible?

In a day when juvenile delinquency is attributed to laxity, sternness, John Dewey, comic books, and world tension—all in one gush of authoritative garrulousness—it would be pointless to attempt an omnibus answer. However, it is conceivable, even probable, that the reader of these tales will himself discern clues to the mentality of rascality. I have detected many in the regal roguishness of Richard Whitney, the spectacular pretensions of Cassie Chadwick, the sexy tomfoolery of "Goat-Gland" Brinkley, and in the antics of other scandalous scamps who were always too ready to prey.

Contents

THE SCANDALOUS SCAMPS

CHAPTER I

The Two Faces of Richard Whitney

W HEN RICHARD WHITNEY fell off his solid gold pedestal, he shattered the tea-cups of the Four Hundred. America's wealthiest families were astounded, for he went from the gray stone of Wall Street up the Hudson River to the red brick of Sing Sing. That was an unpardonable offense, as J. P. Morgan immediately made clear.

"Do you know Richard Whitney?" the banker was asked.

"I *knew* him," Morgan replied, and everyone understood that Whitney had been excommunicated from the temple of high finance.

Richard Whitney was an all-American boy, patrician division. His forebears arrived with the Pilgrims and he arrived when he was included in The Social Register. He sat in exclusive schools, then sat in exclusive clubs. He began at the top in business and ultimately became the leader of an enclosed community of wealth, the New York Stock Exchange. Among his possessions were a country estate, a town house, eight automobiles, forty-seven suits, twelve walking sticks, and four pink coats for fox hunting. On his day of judgment, he had to teach low-brow accountants the proper nomenclature for champagne-bottle sizes. "Gentlemen," he pointed out, "they're not two-quart and six-quart bottles. They're magnums and jeroboams." Ignorance of the social graces appalled him.

In addition to being almost a religious disciple of rugged individualism, Whitney was a crusading foe of shady stock brokers. His vehement denunciations, delivered in a huge number of after-dinner speeches and radio addresses, provided solid assurance to investors. If the law was sometimes the stock swindlers' hellfire, Whitney was their brimstone.

But there were, indeed, two faces of Richard Whitney, for he led a double existence that deceived even those who were closest to him. He swindled during a dozen of his twenty years of prominence in Wall Street. He valued family, caste, and privilege, but he stole from his father-in-law, from his yacht club, from his customers, and his friends. He dealt in enormous financial propositions, but his business judgment was incredibly poor. His pride was devastating, yet when he finally stood morally naked before the world in March, 1938, he delivered himself to his captors, his inferiors, with staggering detachment; it was as if he and the prosecutors and the lawyers and the judges and the prison guards were all talking about somebody else.

As a character in fiction, Whitney would defy belief. He almost does as fact.

Few men could have been better cast for the role Whitney assumed on a morning of lingering chill in May, 1930. At the age of forty-one, he became the youngest president the Stock Exchange had ever known. True, today's ideal market spokesman should exemplify the possibility of ascending from rags to riches, but in 1930, the Big Board was more exclusive. Its face to other worlds, such as the public's, was appropriately one of breeding and manners.

Whitney had those. The son of a Boston banker—unrelated to the more famous Whitney clan—he had been captain of the baseball and football teams at Groton and manager of the school play. His financial bent was recognized when he was made treasurer of the prep school's summer camp. He was no campus clod at Harvard, either, becoming treasurer of Hasty Pudding and pulling a strong oar in the shell that beat Yale in 1909.

Psychiatrists have since revealed certain Whitney characteristics that help illustrate the kind of student he was. He had an utterly factual mind—the kind that a quarter of a century later enabled him to recall, with satisfaction, the full name of every Harvard classmate. But he was no pedant. Philosophical concepts bored him and abstractions repelled him; he paid attention to practical problems, such as campus activities and popularity.

Which probably explains why Dick Whitney made more of a splash at Harvard than had his brother George, who preceded him there and then led the way to Wall Street. George was bookwormish, Dick was raccoon.

But for all that, George was to be the Whitney strength, Dick the family trial. By 1916, George was preparing to become a partner in J. P. Morgan and Company. That year, Dick married Gertrude Sheldon Sands, widow of a son of Mrs. William K. Vanderbilt, and decided to buy a seat on the New York Stock Exchange. It was understandable that he didn't want to borrow so quickly from father-in-law George Sheldon, president of the Union League Club and treasurer of the Republican National Committee, so he tapped an uncle for the price of the seat and established himself as a bond broker.

Whitney quickly generated respect, if not idolatry. Aggressive, assured, he drove with authority toward the Exchange's inner circle. He had a sharp tongue, a short manner, and no time for nonsense, which included almost anything not connected with business. Some associates thought him unduly grim, but most were content that he gave so much time to organizational affairs. He soon became a member of the Exchange's governing committee, a post he held until the day of his expulsion. He sat with the committee on business conduct (that is, misconduct) and eventually became its chairman. In 1928 he was elected vice-president of the most powerful securities exchange in the world.

That was the progress registered by one Richard Whitney. Another Richard Whitney, carrying on in the same body, was meanwhile having a devil of a time keeping his own house as tidy as he did the Big Board's. This, despite his acknowledged position as the leader of the "bond crowd." He was known as the Morgan broker, because he handled approximately thirty percent of the bond orders placed by J. P. Morgan and Company, where brother George spent his days. This fraternal arrangement netted Dick Whitney $50,000 a year in commissions.

The problem was that Dick had been infected by a speculative bug that constantly diverted his attention from the ploddingly gainful bond business. Early in the exuberant 1920's, for instance, he was attracted by a Florida company that wanted to transform humus into a commercial fertilizer. He began investing an average of $200,000 a year. Then he saw possibilities in a firm organized to mine and sell mineral colloids. He didn't have enough liquid cash for such investments, but he did have enthusiasm, so brother George made him a series of loans that came to $575,000 for these two flings alone.

George could afford it; whether he worried about payment is unknown. It is also difficult to know if he wondered about Richard's judgment, or merely thought it not cricket to pry. As he explained later, "If my brother was to borrow, it was better that he should borrow from me."

But Richard's investment ventures failed to justify hopes and his neglected bond business was suddenly in deep crisis. Some men fold up under extreme pressure, while others drive to Himalayas of resourcefulness. Whitney was resourceful. Scouring his office vault for stray assets, he came onto $105,000 in stocks belonging to the account of his father-in-law; Sheldon had died, and Whitney was an administrator of his estate. He hurried over to the Corn Exchange Bank and put up the trust securities as collateral for a loan. It was to be a temporary device, to alleviate his crisis, and it is probable that his narrowly focused mind did not associate his action with criminal conduct. But it is another matter whether his failure to make this association stemmed from thoroughgoing honesty or from a snobbish conviction that society's laws did not really apply to rich people.

In any event, Richard Whitney broke the honesty habit, consciously or not. If he was slightly nervous at the next meeting of the committee on business conduct, at least it was not because his firm was in peril. In fact, he felt secure enough to relocate Richard Whitney and Company in fifteen rooms of a new building on Broad Street, where his private office overlooked the Stock Exchange.

When some costly stock speculations created a new peril only two years later, the Sheldon securities were still in hock. Such things have a way of happening, as any practiced embezzler could have told Whitney. To meet the new crisis, he mortgaged his upper East Side town house for $110,000, thus taking the first step on a treadmill of interest payments that would eventually exhaust him. Like a poor man visiting a loan shark with desperate regularity, the boy from Groton and Harvard became a moneylender's dream.

Those were the dissimilar achievements of the two Richard Whitneys—the vice-president of the New York Stock Exchange and the bumbling businessman—as America turned into 1929, the climactic year of the era of wonderful nonsense.

Investors had been watching the financial bubble expand, hearing that stock prices were still lower than true values, buying such issues as RCA—which rose from $85 a share to $420 in twelve months without ever having paid a dividend. Exhilaration was so intense that sporadic spring and summer turndowns worried few people. But, familiarly enough, the situation became alarmingly clear by October, when the market sagged under hammering blows of selling. Down in Wall Street, the big bankers conferred and J. P. Morgan decreed that the market had to be supported. A social expression of heredity was at work; twenty-two years earlier, in the financial panic of 1907, Morgan's father had organized the support of several failing banks.

So it was that in mid-October, the duality of Richard Whitney's life was accented once more. On the one hand, caught up in the possibilities of the frenzied price rise, he had borrowed more money from brother George with which to buy another seat on the Exchange and he had increased his personal investments heavily. On the other hand, the president of the Exchange, Edward H. H. Simmons, was off in Europe and Whitney found himself the market's chief officer, the instrument of authority in the whirl of panic.

On October 24, Black Thursday of 1929, with investors' margin accounts expiring under the heaviest price slide in securities history, Whitney enacted the role that would make him famous and set his future course even more decisively. At one-thirty P.M. he interrupted the near hysteria that gripped the Exchange floor by appearing from the members' lobby and walking slowly toward Trading Post No. 2, where transactions in the stock of United States Steel were handled. As more and more brokers noticed him a buzz arose; by the time he reached the circular trading post, a thousand pairs of eyes abandoned the high, illuminated tickers and fixed on his commanding frame. No one had to explain the significance of his rare appearance on the floor. The Morgan broker had arrived. In his hand was a slip of paper. The bankers were making their move. Whitney was their emissary.

"205 for Steel!" he called. Then he placed orders with the steel-stock specialist for 10,000 shares at that price— a commitment of over $2,000,000. Since $205 was the price of the last previous sale in Steel, it was obvious that the bankers had decided to shore up the market. But more, Whitney then toured to several other trading posts and, with studied lack of haste, placed $25,000,000 more in orders for fifteen to twenty other stocks, in 10,000-share blocks.

The gesture was temporarily effective. For the first time in days the selling wave abated. The ticker, tardily announcing the demise of fortunes that had vanished hours earlier, began catching up. Prices firmed and, as a matter of fact, Whitney's demand for 10,000 shares of Steel at 205 was met by only two hundred shares. Who knew but that the price direction might be ready to reverse?

But history, economics, or whatever dynamic had already sealed the fate of the Stock Market continued the irreversible pressure. The market went on to crash, the experts gulped, and the Great Depression settled on the land. Whitney lost $2,000,000 in the collapse, or so he said, and friends later advanced this misfortune as his motivation for embezzling. But other men lost money in the crash too, other men who were not already living two lives.

Out of the wreckage of October and November emerged a hero, a man who had selflessly abandoned his own affairs to work with the bankers and try to save the market. In May, 1930, the brokers crackled with appreciation and elected Richard Whitney president of the Stock Exchange. They also presented him with a touching souvenir—Trading Post No. 2, the Steel post at which he had tried to redirect history. He installed it in the lobby of his Broad Street offices, where it became a Wall Street memento.

The other Richard Whitney, the beggar on horseback, was deeper into George's wallet by then, having borrowed

more money with which to reorganize his firm into a
partnership. It was a strange partnership; despite the addition of four new members, Richard Whitney and Company was a one-man firm. A discerning Morgan man referred to Whitney's colleagues as "office boys" and
suggested that stronger partners be brought in to curb the
bond broker's speculative imagination. But Whitney preferred his office boys. He never called a partners' meeting
and no partners were consulted when he committed the
firm to huge loans. He ignored them in the same way he
ignored as much of the world as he could.

But he could not ignore his sinking fortunes. By now,
he was paying fantastic interest on his multifarious loans—
and the compensating returns were meager. Humus wasn't
making out and neither were the mineral colloids. So, no
sooner did he become president of the Exchange than his
new firm was in trouble. Again the man demonstrated his
resourcefulness. He had been elected treasurer of the New
York Yacht Club, which brought him into possession of
over $100,000 worth of securities. In May, June, and July
of 1930, he used the Yacht Club's bonds in an ungentle-
manly way. With them, he floated thirteen separate loans,
using one to pay off another as quickly as they could be
arranged, and thus he saved himself from drowning.

A year later his position was still critical and again one
Richard Whitney was able to save the other. Having
become a director of the Corn Exchange Bank, he appreciated the difficulty fellow directors would have in turning
him down, and asked for a loan of $300,000. He offered
no collateral and they requested none. He got the money,
as he was fond of saying, on his face. It may be that the
bankers subscribed to the homily of the elder J. P. Morgan,

who resolutely held that a man's character was worth more than his collateral.

But one Corn Exchange director, a Morgan partner named Francis Bartow, was unhappy over the transaction. He did not consider Whitney's action improper, he said, but felt that others might misunderstand it. Appearances must have counted heavily with Bartow, because he reported his apprehension to George Whitney. Shortly afterward, the loan was quietly picked up by the House of Morgan—thus keeping it in the family closet. The Morgan partners naturally placed utmost confidence in character and they, too, asked Whitney for no collateral.

Under the circumstances, the President of the Stock Exchange was reasonably free from harassment for the next couple of years, finding it necessary to appropriate his father-in-law's securities only once more. He was living well on his country estate, a 495-acre gentleman's farm at Far Hills, New Jersey, where he was a member of the township committee, a leader of the so-called New York Colony, and master of the foxhounds at the Essex Hunt. His farm payroll came to $1,500 a month, for a superintendent, herdsmen, grooms, a jockey, a gardener, and teamsters. Who else could care properly for his horses, his prize Ayrshire chickens, and his thoroughbred Berkshire pigs? Certainly not the butler, whose hands were full of magnums and jeroboams of champagne.

If times make the man, this period made Whitney. He became the acknowledged spokesman for the policies and practices of the New York Stock Exchange. He was its depression president as Franklin Roosevelt, a contrasting product of Groton and Harvard, was the nation's depression president.

Whitney despised the New Deal, and the New Deal despised the private-club nature of the Stock Exchange. He railed at the braintrusters, warning them to keep their governmental regulators away from the securities market. He made speeches, testified before Congressional committees, and otherwise confirmed his leadership of the Old Guard among the men of the market. Some of the younger crowd felt that the reform mood of the nation called for compromise, but they got Whitney's sharp tongue for their trouble.

The New Deal surged forward under Roosevelt's huge Congressional majority and one day Whitney sat in the Senate gallery as final approval was given a bill creating the Securities and Exchange Commission. To him, an SEC was socialistic and he returned to New York with his blue blood high in adrenalin.

That was in 1934, and the men named Richard Whitney must have found a way to get twenty-six hours out of a day. While spokesman Whitney was spending his evenings on podiums, businessman Whitney had been paying out almost a quarter of a million dollars in interest on his multiple loans. He owed George almost $2,000,000 and was in so deep that when he borrowed $110,000 from a friend for thirty days (without collateral), the loan ran forty-three months before he paid up at the insistence of the friend's partner.

Despite his already dangerous position, Whitney started down an even riskier path. When repeal of Prohibition was just around the corner, he had become attracted to the Distilled Liquors Corporation, a firm organized to produce applejack. A lot has been said for and against diversification of holdings, but the case of "Applejack" Richard Whitney at least provides dramatic proof of the danger of putting all your borrowed dollars into one liquor bottle.

When Distilled Liquors floated its first stock issue, Whitney bought 15,000 shares at $15. That cost him $225,000, most of which he borrowed. Then he watched DLC's price rise until it hit $45. Some men might have taken their profit of almost a half million dollars and run. Not Whitney. Since his need for funds was gargantuan, he pledged the stock as collateral for still more bank loans.

The securities, however, were destined for disaster. They sold well but the applejack didn't. Partly on Whitney's advice, the company expanded production and enlarged its sales organization. When that failed to help, it added a line of rye whisky, which didn't go either. The firm was losing money at the rate of $55,000 a year and, as this news inevitably reached Wall Street, where the pulse of a corporation is taken through its balance sheet, the stock's price slipped. Nothing could have injured Whitney's position more. If DLC's price fell, so would its value as loan collateral; next would come the dreaded bank call for repayment or additional collateral.

So Whitney was forced to compound his debts and to hasten his own exposure. In an effort to keep DLC's price pegged at a level that would protect it as collateral, he began buying heavily. He bought until he owned 75,000 shares. The price continued to drop and, frantically, he bought more. There was no need for resourcefulness now; he simply had a bear by the tail and couldn't let go without losing everything. He used clients' securities, the Sheldon estate, the New York Yacht Club bonds, his wife's jewelry, and whatever else he could grasp and hold onto long enough to hock. All of it went into collateral for bank loans that would either buy more DLC stock or repay other bank loans that had already been used to buy the stock. Personal, unsecured loans from other brokers added to the niagara of debt and interest. It was an incredible juggling operation, a nerve-racking procedure that was not only illegal but a sure path, barring a miracle, to insolvency and jail.

If this occurred to Richard Whitney the businessman, it was not obvious in the actions of Richard Whitney the president of the New York Stock Exchange. He continued to denounce brokers who suggested coming to terms with the New Dealers and he warned the man in the street to beware the bucket-shop swindlers. He told a national radio audience that investors should deal only with "financial houses of established responsibility, houses whose operations are controlled not only by law, but by their own pride in fair dealing."

By May, 1935, when he gave up the Stock Exchange presidency, Whitney had lost over $400,000 in speculations other than the Distilled Liquors venture. And DLC was still sliding, even though he had aggregated more than 100,000 shares. Desperately, he pledged $250,000 worth of life insurance policies as collateral for fresh loans.

The climax, a tortuous, yearlong affair, began developing the spring of 1937 when Whitney visited his brother George and told him of a fresh difficulty. It had familiar overtones. He had received permission from three friends to pledge their securities for bank loans, but now the friends wanted their securities back and he was in no position to oblige them. So George put up $1,225,000 to make this possible and Richard paid up the loans and got the stock back. He was supposed to return it to his vaults, since his firm held the three brokerage accounts in question, but instead he took the securities to another bank and pledged them all over again. His bank loans now totaled over $5,000,000 but that figure had only a limited meaning, since some loans merely paid off others in a bewildering race against due dates.

The pace of Whitney's demise was quickened, unknowingly, by the New York Stock Exchange itself. Among the official positions he held after leaving the presidency of the Big Board was one as a trustee of the Gratuity Fund, a trust for which members were taxed and which was used to benefit their widows and orphans. The Fund consisted of $2,000,000 in bonds and cash, and Richard Whitney and Company handled its investment transactions under the direction of the trustees.

Early in 1937, the trustees voted that two blocks of bonds should be sold and a $175,000-block purchased. The bonds were sent over to Whitney's office and the deal was made. Instead of returning the $175,000 in new bonds and a cash remainder, however, he kept them. Then bonds worth $225,000 more found their way into Whitney vaults by the same method. By October, he held $900,000 in bonds and $221,000 in cash belonging to the Fund.

While he had devotedly attended every meeting of the Gratuity Fund trustees, for some reason he was unable to attend a session that took place on Monday, November 22. Near the close of that meeting, George W. Lutes, a clerk for the trustees, remarked casually that Whitney had not returned the securities and cash. He also said he had reminded the broker of this fact five times in six months. Later, Lutes and an investigator for the Securities and Exchange Commission engaged in this exchange:

Q. As the months rolled by, Mr. Lutes, didn't you talk to him a little more vigorously about those bonds?

A. Absolutely not, because Mr. Whitney was a more or less sharp person, and I could not go up to him and say, "Here, Mr. Whitney, you send those bonds over to us," or anything of that sort, because Mr. Whitney was my superior. I was under him as an employee of the Exchange and I am only a clerk of the committee.

Q. Were you concerned about your job, Mr. Lutes?

A. Certainly.

When Lutes made his revelation at the November 22 meeting, Edward Simmons, the trustees' chairman, accused the $43.50-a-week clerk of inefficiency. Simmons finally turned his attention to the higher-priced malefactor. He called Whitney's office and was assured that the securities and cash would be returned forthwith.

The following morning, Tuesday, Whitney dropped in on Simmons and agreed that the holdings should really be in a bank vault. He said his office would try to deliver them that day, but that he was shorthanded at the moment. Simmons, who knew that that was one of the reasons Whitney had given Lutes for his earlier failures to return the assets, insisted he have them by three o'clock that afternoon. Whitney said he would do his best.

But his best would not be good enough, for a certainty. He had already put up two-thirds of the $900,000 in securities as collateral for loans. Moreover, he had only $74,000 in cash to cover the Fund's $221,000. The shortage was formidable.

Whitney ran his only course. Mortification before

brother George was preferable to public exposure, so he hurried to George and told all. George was properly aghast. Exactly what was said between them remains a mystery, but George, who didn't have a large amount of cash on hand, went to another Morgan partner, Thomas W. Lamont, and despite differences in later recollections, told him at least enough to borrow $1,082,000.

When Whitney called on Simmons at the three P.M. deadline, he said the securities would be returned the next day and added, for reassurance, that he had "talked with George." Simmons, now concerned over the significance of Whitney's inability to hand over the securities and cash at once, called George Whitney himself and received Morgan-type assurances. On Wednesday the sum was returned and—officially, at least—the matter was closed. The record of a subsequent meeting of the Gratuity Fund trustees states that "all securities of the trustees held by Richard Whitney & Company have been received and placed in the vault, and the cash balance of the trustees held by Richard Whitney & Company has been turned over to the trustees and placed in the bank." The widows and orphans were safe.

Privately, however, the matter was wide open. On Thursday, Thanksgiving Day, two meetings were held at George Whitney's home. At a morning session, the Whitney brothers conferred with Edward Simmons. At an afternoon session only the brothers were present. When Richard left that evening, it was with the understanding that his company would liquidate. George had suffered enough. Conceivably, he might have carried Dick till doomsday with loans that had taken on the character of outright gifts, but the revelations of the morning session, when he and Simmons had pried deeply into Dick's affairs, were too much. The pattern was clear; Whitney had been appropriating money wherever he could. The only way to avoid a public debacle was to get him out of Wall Street in an "orderly" way.

If the way could have been made orderly, the world might never have known about the other face of Richard Whitney. Like the bank teller who returns from the race-track with his winnings and erases the faint pencil nota-tions of his temporary embezzlement, Whitney's depreda-tions might have gone forever undetected. But he had rarely won and was still losing heavily. His Distilled Liquors stock was down from 45 to 11 and he was out a million dollars there. He had mortgaged his New Jersey estate for $250,000, which added to interest payments that were already grotesque. Frantically, he tried to borrow from everyone who crossed his erratic path and often succeeded, despite the fact that gossip was getting about.

His exposure, like many great discoveries, came about accidentally. The catalyst was a change of policy by the Stock Exchange's governors. For some time they had re-quired financial reports only from brokers who carried the public's margin accounts. Whitney, a broker's broker, having little to do with public investors, had been exempt from filling out a questionnaire that would have revealed his condition. But late in 1937, it was decided that all brokerage houses should report.

Coincidentally, Whitney approached Bernard E. Smith, the legendary short-seller, and asked for $250,000. Instead of offering collateral, he again used the expression "on my face." Smith, who had rarely received a tip of the hat from

Whitney, told him he didn't like his face and reported the incident to Charles R. Gay, the Exchange president. Then another broker picked up a rumor that Greyhound Bus stock was involved in distress selling and that Whitney was the seller. Since distress selling meant an order to sell regardless of the market price, it connoted severe financial trouble, and the broker dutifully reported the rumor to the chairman of the committee on business conduct. As it turned out later, the rumor was false; there were no distress sales of Greyhound stock. But the wheels began grinding. The business conduct committee, being at least tacitly aware of the Gratuity Fund incident, decided to send Whitney a financial questionnaire without delay.

The caged broker now fairly flew between banks and individuals. He pledged $800,000 more in customers' securities in order to raise cash and buy another 40,000 shares of Distilled Liquors stock, hoping to send its price up and recoup everything. It stayed down; in fact, during January and February he was DLC's sole purchaser. To disguise his heavy involvement with one security, he put thousands of shares in his partners' names and, since they had never developed the habit of questioning his conduct, they said nothing.

After a week's delay, Whitney delivered his questionnaire. Despite all the deceit it contained, he could not make it show sufficient operating capital under Stock Exchange rules. An audit of his books was immediately ordered and by March 1 the auditor reported evidence of extensive misappropriations. On that day, Whitney went to W. Averell Harriman, later a national figure and governor of New York, then a partner in Brown Brothers Harriman and Co., and asked for $100,000. He said he had no collateral at the moment but would deliver securities in a few days. He got the money but Harriman didn't get the collateral.

If that loan seems extraordinary, consider that in the four months between November, 1937 and March, 1938, Whitney floated no less than 111 loans totaling $27,000,-000. He was in a revolving door that threatened at each turn to trap him.

On Saturday, March 5, Whitney spent a remarkable two hours with President Gay of the Stock Exchange while the members of the committee on business conduct were preparing charges against him. He neither begged nor pleaded, but was businesslike and, above all, practical. Pointing out the Exchange would receive adverse publicity if he were exposed, he offered to relinquish his membership and leave the Street. Gay said no. Whitney remained emotionless, continuing the negotiations as if he were a lawyer for someone else in trouble. Then he left, knowing he was finished, and waited calmly for the formal blow to fall.

The last effort to save him, or to save the Whitney name, was made on Sunday. Francis Bartow, the Morgan partner, spent that afternoon discussing the affair with other Morgan men, not including George Whitney, who was in Florida because of ill health. On Sunday evening, Bartow drove out to the Long Island home of John W. Davis, the Morgan attorney who had been the Democratic presidential candidate in 1924. Davis flatly prohibited giving financial help on grounds that, with Whitney facing criminal action, the Morgan firm's motives might be misconstrued. Bartow phoned George Whitney in

Florida, but told him there was no point in his returning; nothing could be done to save Dick.

On Monday morning, Bartow returned to Long Island, this time to make a final appeal to J. P. Morgan himself. But Morgan stood with Davis.

On Tuesday, March 8, after the clang of the opening bell, President Gay appeared on the elevated rostrum at one end of the Stock Exchange floor. The brokers turned to him and heard the terrible news: Richard Whitney and Company had been suspended for insolvency.

That was politeness in the extreme, on a par with the Exchange's news release that spoke of Whitney's "conduct apparently contrary to just and equitable principles of trade."

District Attorney Thomas E. Dewey quickly obtained a New York County indictment charging Whitney with having embezzled $105,000 from the estate of his father-in-law. Richard's total deficit was $5,600,000, of which brother George Whitney was on the short end by $2,897,-000.

Arrested, Whitney stood in court, hands clasped behind a fitted overcoat with velvet collar, and was arraigned. Then he was taken to a police station on the lower East Side for booking. A group of Bowery derelicts was herded into a back room for the occasion and Whitney was brought before a desk sergeant who was clearly nonplused by the tall, gray, dignified figure before him. Awkwardly, he asked if the prisoner had been seached.

An officer stammered, "Not yet." Whitney smiled and opened his coat. "Have you got any knives?" a policeman asked.

"No," he replied.

The desk sergeant stood up, reached over, and extended a hand. "Mr. Whitney," he said, "I'm sorry to see you in this trouble and I wish you the best of luck."

Whitney shook the hand and said, "Thank you."

The sergeant started to sit down, then stopped. "The Whitneys have always had a good name," he said. Then, perhaps on the suspicion that he had offended, he sat down hard.

"Thank you again," Whitney said. He was mugged, fingerprinted, and released on $10,000 bail.

A few days later, when the state indicted him, too—for misusing $120,000 in bonds of the New York Yacht Club —a judge held court open until five P.M., so the prisoner wouldn't have to spend a night in jail before arraignment. "I'm sorry for your trouble," he told Whitney.

A week later the broker was expelled from the Stock Exchange. Then he pleaded guilty to the combined indictments and received a five-to-ten year prison sentence. He was handcuffed to a rapist and sent up to Warden Lewis E. Lawes at Sing Sing, where a problem of deportment developed. Convicts tipped their caps, stepped aside as he passed, and addressed him as Mr. Whitney. A guard called out, "All men who came in Saturday, Monday, or Tuesday, and Mr. Whitney, please step out of the cells." But the novelty soon passed, and normalcy prevailed once more.

The real problems, the social ripples that started with Whitney's arrest, spread rapidly across the nation. There was resentment that a gigantic swindler had been indicted for only two of his numerous larcenies and that he could be paroled in less than three and a half years. The depth of this feeling was illustrated by a St. Louis judge who was sentencing a young man for stealing two dollars from a filling station. "Some people think there's one law for the rich and another for the poor," the judge said. "We'll correct that right now."

Taking pencil and paper, he made elaborate computations and then said, "Richard Whitney got five years for stealing $225,000. That would be $45,000 a year, $120 a day, five dollars an hour. You stole two dollars. That would be twenty-four minutes and that is your sentence."

The philosophy behind the judge's maverick behavior might have been lost on the prisoner, but it was not lost on others. The New York Stock Exchange became a target for considerable criticism. The Securities and Exchange Commission climaxed its investigation of the case by accusing Stock Exchange officials of having known for months of Whitney's actions and of shielding him with their code of silence. The Commissioners pointed out that he had borrowed over $6,000,000 from sixteen persons connected with the Big Board, that he had been turned down by twenty-one others, and that such wholesale borrowing was an obvious signal of deep-seated trouble.

"Thus," the SEC concluded, "Richard Whitney, as a member of the Stock Exchange fraternity, was able for years to hide his misdeeds behind that code of silence."

Exchange officials, represented by attorney Dean Acheson, steadfastly denied moral guilt and rode out the storm —a storm that was intensified by J. P. Morgan's admission that he would not have informed the authorities of Whitney's actions under any conditions.

Despite this attitude, the private club was indeed changing under the pressure of the times. For the first time in its history, the Exchange appointed a non-broker as president, and added three "public representatives" to its Board of Governors. But eight months after Whitney went to jail, the governors voted twenty-seven to one against reviewing the conduct of their members in the Whitney case. Robert M. Hutchins, president of the University of Chicago and the public-member minority of one, resigned with a public protest. Thereafter, the Exchange just lived with the memory of its fallen leader and hoped others would soon forget.

As for Whitney, he scrubbed cell walls, clerked, played a creditable first base on the Sing Sing ball team, and was paroled, in 1941, after serving three years and four months. George Whitney, who had meanwhile become president of J. P. Morgan and Company, picked him up at the prison gates and saw him off to Massachusetts, where he managed a dairy farm and then rose from apprentice in an explosives plant to become executive assistant to a vice-president. In 1946, at the age of fifty-seven, he became president of a small fiber company not far from Orlando, Florida.

If Whitney has managed to forget, or at least to dim the memory, the New York Stock Exchange is still trying. Today, in the handsomely appointed rooms of its Board of Governors, you can see large oil paintings of its past presidents—all but Whitney. The official explanation of this omission is lack of space. While that may sound like a public relations contortion, the Exchange's rationale does have undeniable logic. Surely two portraits of Richard Whitney would be unthinkable, and one would only tell half the story of a man who lived a double life.

CHAPTER II

"520%" Miller

ON NEW YEAR'S DAY, 1889, William Franklin Miller decided to get rich quick. The sallow, twenty-year-old clerk was motivated by several pressing problems, all of which, he felt, could be solved with money. He had a sick wife and baby, a record of failures in penny ante stock speculations, and a profound sensitivity about his height, or lack of it. Miller stood five feet, five inches tall in patent leather shoes with thick heels, and he imagined that people looked down on him in more ways than one. He knew that all the money in the world couldn't buy him another six inches, but he thought it might purchase some ego.

As a result of these irritations, Miller embarked on an investment scheme that was incredible in its simplicity. He said he had inside tips on the stock market, tips that would make him rich if he but had capital to invest. If investors would provide the capital, he would be grateful enough—and, more importantly, well able—to pay them ten percent interest every week on every dollar they put up. In other words, a return of 520% a year.

He paid it, too, and when he did, depositors fought in

the street before his office for places in line. Men borrowed against their businesses to raise investment funds, and so much money eventually poured in that Miller and his employees had to shovel it into barrels. It simply couldn't be counted.

When the remarkable empire collapsed only eleven months after it was constituted, the crash was heard across the nation and into Canada. Its last echo carried "520%" Miller into Sing Sing Prison, a magnificent faker and a thorough bust, by the time he was old enough to vote.

From the year he could read a Bible, Miller's parents had demanded his unfailing attendance at a Sunday School located near their modest home in the Williamsburg section of Brooklyn. It was only logical, then, that he should choose as his first victims several young men who studied the Bible with him. These youths were sadly cloistered, for when they learned that Miller had worked in Wall Street brokerage houses, they developed the notion that he knew what made the stock tickers tick. He decided not to correct this misconception. Instead, as they listened to theological lectures, he rubbed a bristly blond mustache and wondered how he could put their illusions to work.

As 1899 opened he was prepared and, with his slight stammer, he broached his proposition one freezing morning after Sunday School had let out. If some of the young men would give him ten dollars, he said, his inside tips would earn them a return of one dollar each week. In ten weeks they would have their principal back and then, nothing but astronomical profits. The inducement was tempting enough and half the class, or ten ten-dollar men, elected to beat Wall Street with "520%" Miller.

The young promoter was delighted. His wispiness gave way before a brass-nerved plan that was as cunning as it was crooked. He had no inside tips on the stock market and did not intend to invest a cent of the hundred dollars he had collected. He would merely pocket it and pay the ten dollar weekly interest out of principal paid by new depositors. So long as he could turn up fresh ten dollar investors, and get the old ones to add more ten dollar bills, the one dollar interest payments would take care of themselves handily and he would soon be wealthy. If a day of reckoning lay somewhere in the future of such a scheme, it was not visible to Miller.

He quit his job and spent his days making collections and soliciting new business. From house to house through Brooklyn he trudged, with his office in his black derby. In his spare time, when he was supposedly scouting hot stocks, he was counting his money. And as word of his phenomenal returns spread, the amount to be counted rose each week.

Business so boomed that by the middle of February, Miller couldn't keep up with his daily rounds. Moreover, he quickly reached that critical point in the careers of rascals at which they begin mistaking their own boloney for good steak; he felt it had become undignified for William Franklin Miller to tramp around after money. So he rented a room in a ramshackle two-story frame house on Floyd Street and announced that he would receive investors there or not at all.

His new leisure time gave Miller's frustrated creativeness an opportunity to flourish. He wrote vivid, golden-egg circulars that would entice investors from far beyond the limits of Brooklyn. He poured persuasive nonsense

into weekly newsletters and mailed them south as far as
Louisiana and north to Manitoba. Feeling then that his
enterprise needed a title with more timbre, he took his
own middle name, embellished it with a photograph of
another Franklin (a man named Benjamin), and declared
himself the "Franklin Syndicate." His motto was also
Ben Franklin's: "The way to wealth is as plain as the road
to the market."

One newsletter explained his mammoth interest payments
with an air of intrigue, yet logic:

This may look impossible to you, but you know there must
be a way where one can double his money in a short time or
else there should be no Jay Gould, Vanderbilt and other
millionaires who have made their fortunes in Wall Street after
starting with almost nothing.

Another newsletter offered a thrill that few speculators
could resist. Miller made them part of a gigantic stock-
tipping operation. "My ambition," he said, "is to make the
Franklin Syndicate one of the largest and strongest operating in Wall Street, which will enable us to manipulate
stocks, putting them up or down as we desire. That will
make our profits five times more than they are now."

Could the key to the U. S. Treasury seem more beguiling? Apparently not; the dream of beating Wall Street is
even more fetching than that of winning the Daily Double
and taking a taxi home from the racetrack. The investors
flocked to his door, and Miller set Friday as the day
deposits had to be made in order to receive interest the
following week.

So Friday became carnival day at the house on Floyd
Street. Crowds lined up waiting for the office to open and,
as they swelled each week, the police closed the street to

traffic. More than one policeman joined the line, and the presence of New York's Finest gave investors a feeling of security. While the bluecoats waited to turn over their money, they broke up scuffles among the impatient.

Just inside the doors at the top of the front steps, Miller sat at a desk, rubbing his mustache nervously with one hand as he signed little pink and green receipts with the other. He became so pressed by demands for his attention that he hired a boy to help him and then had to put on four clerks as well.

By the coming of spring, no man could sign his name as many times a day as 520% Miller had to. He had a rubber stamp made of his neat, round-lettered signature, and he rented all the rooms on the upper floor of the house. Soon he occupied the whole building.

Which is not to say that Miller was entirely without critics. Pay what return you will, make what miracles you wish, there will always be someone to doubt you. One such skeptic was the pastor of the Congregational Church to which Miller belonged. When he became aware of the pagan amounts of money his Sunday School student was garnering, he expelled him from the church straightaway and asked the police to take him in as a crook.

A lieutenant replied, "I don't know that I'd be able to arrest the man even if I did get a complaint. Most of my patrolmen, inspectors, and detectives seem to be in it, and I'm thinking seriously of going in next week myself."

The minister retreated in pain and shock.

Unaware of such examples of mistrust, out-of-towners were making sure they were not excluded from New York's financial bonanza. Their money-stuffed letters began to arrive in wagonloads. Four clerks in the Central

Brooklyn Post Office were assigned to the exclusive duty of handling Franklin Syndicate mail. Miller gasped the first day that three mail wagons pulled up in Floyd Street together, but he regained calm quickly enough and expanded his clerking force to fifty. Even this number could not possibly count all the money, so they threw it onto the floor behind them as fast as it was received. At the end of the day they shoveled green bills and gold coins into barrels at the back of the house. Some undoubtedly pilfered bills, too, but since Miller kept no accounting system, this never became an issue. Besides, it just didn't matter.

"We opened early and closed at ten P.M.," he said later, "but we never got through counting the cash until three o'clock in the morning. On Saturday mornings, we rarely concluded the task before daylight."

Success stimulated the young man's latent sense of the dramatic. He decided to open the Floyd Street doors and let the investors come all the way into the gold mine. He placed two roll-top desks at the far end of the parlor. That was where deposits would be received. But in order to reach those desks, depositors had to pass a glass-windowed booth at which the interest payments were made. The size of the payments so excited them that, by the time they reached the roll-top desks, many doubled and tripled the amounts they came to invest.

And similarly, those who were receiving payments at the interest booth became so exhilarated by the sight of steady lines of waiting depositors that, instead of collecting their interest, they redeposited it to be added to the principal they had already sunk in. It was a splendid display of the power of visual excitation.

This development so snowballed the number of investors that Miller was forced to take a drastic step. He turned every room in the house into an office and, before long, money was being received everywhere from the kitchen to the bathrooms. Like a torrent, money was raining all over William Franklin Miller. He had never earned over five dollars a week in any previous endeavor; now he went to a Fifth Avenue tailor and came away with $1,800 worth of clothes.

Then the newly minted tycoon was chagrined when an investor asked him why so affluent a syndicate was quartered in such a dingy house. He thought this over, and made an explanation in a newsletter that damned the high overhead of the plush Wall Street brokerage houses.

"Your money buys neither mahogany desks nor oil paintings," he said. "It is put to work for you at ten percent a week. Our running expenses are small, our profits enormous and sure."

That was received with grins of satisfaction, followed by sneers at the Wall Street brokers—brokers who couldn't pay anything like 520% interest a year. The number of depositors continued to rise until Miller was forced to take another drastic step. In mid-October, he issued this notice:

Our business has increased to such an extent that we find ourselves unable to accept deposits under fifty dollars, lesser sums causing a congestion of detail that hardly pays us to handle these small amounts.

No matter how successful the enterprise seemed, the press remained singularly skeptical. Newspapers could not explain how the Franklin Syndicate was operating, but neither could they bring themselves to swallow the scheme. Some hinted broadly that swindle was in the air, but few readers got the message. As for Miller, he explained away such deprecation as green-eyed jealousy of a man who had found a sure-fire way to beat the system.

His confidence surged, and he opened a branch office in Boston for the convenience of the multitudes of that city. He looked up a fly-by-night stock operator, Edward Schlessinger, made him a partner, and established him in Boston. But the office had no sooner opened than the Boston *Post* openly denounced the Syndicate as a swindler's paradise. Miller felt the first stirrings of panic. He conferred with an advertising man he had hired and was told to contact a New York lawyer named Robert Adams Ammon, known in legal—and illegal—circles as "Colonel" Ammon.

Miller found in Ammon everything he wasn't and couldn't really become. He had convinced many people that he was a self-assured figure of authority but, at heart, he knew he was a scurrying mouse. Ammon, on the other hand, was tall, strapping, and genuinely bluff-mannered. He cockily epitomized the man of confidence. Moreover, he was a veteran at skirmishing with the statute books over questionable stock-selling enterprises.

Colonel Ammon told Miller to leave everything to him. First, he said, they would go to Boston and prepare for an investors' run on the branch office. Miller stuffed $70,000 in five dollar bills into a suitcase and they left. As Ammon had anticipated, the depositors who read the *Post* swarmed the office, demanding refunds. Miller was glad he had retained Ammon, for while the Colonel's plan cost him $28,000, the gesture was immediately effective. It stopped the run and restored confidence. Ammon took a $5,000 fee out of what remained in the suitcase and the pair returned to New York.

This brief run started, and was stopped, in mid-November, 1899—but Ammon, at least, saw the handwriting on the wall. He knew the Syndicate could not last much longer and decided to cut himself a quick and large slice of the money pie. He selected the week beginning Monday, November 20, for the feast and he made it the most suspenseful week of Miller's young but hectic life.

On Monday, Ammon advised that the time had come to hit the investors hard. Accordingly, Miller composed a telegram and sent it to all depositors. It read:

WE HAVE INSIDE INFORMATION ON BIG TRANS-ACTION TO BEGIN SATURDAY OR MONDAY MORNING. BIG PROFITS. REMIT AT ONCE TO RECEIVE THE PROFITS.   —W. F. MILLER

He added a touch of his own—a cheap touch that he couldn't resist. He sent the telegrams collect.

On Tuesday, Miller was greeted at the Brooklyn offices by Edward Schlessinger. The Boston branch manager allowed that things were getting too warm up there. He crammed $175,000 into a valise, said good-by, and boarded a ship for Europe. Miller, who did not feel up to asking the police to stop him, let him go quietly and waited impatiently for the weekend.

On Wednesday, about 1,000 telegrams for which investors had refused to pay were returned. But when the mail arrived later in the day, it was stuffed with cash from the faithful majority.

On Thursday, Miller sweated out more mail at Floyd Street, then panicked. He took $30,500 and went to Ammon's office in lower Manhattan. Ammon told him to prepare to flee to Canada and to turn over to him the money that Miller held in various banks. They went to the Wells Fargo bank, where Ammon deposited the $30,500 in his own account, together with a deposit receipt for $100,000 that Miller had previously banked. Miller also gave him a check for $10,000 and an order for $40,000 more in government bonds. Instructing the jittery youth to go home to his wife, Ammon went to his ornate house on Staten Island with bank receipts representing $180,500 of Miller's holdings.

On Friday Miller went to his office and picked up more money. A brief fight broke out at six P.M. when a man tried to deposit $150 and was told the Syndicate had closed for the day. When Miller's clerks agreed to take fifty dollars, the man went away quietly.

On Saturday, Miller came into Floyd Street and saw a huge crowd. He slipped into the house and remained in a back room until one P.M., when he started for home. Suspecting he was being followed, he boarded a streetcar, got off a block later, dodged through a drug store and a Chinese laundry, raced onto an elevated train, and dashed into Ammon's office at two P.M. As he entered, Ammon was receiving a telephone message that the Brooklyn Grand Jury had finally indicted Miller for conspiracy to defraud.

The lawyer rose and placed a steadying hand on his client's shoulder. "My boy," he said, "there's nothing to worry about. But you'll have to leave for Canada right now. I'll send your wife and baby later." Miller departed, taking that day's receipts with him.

The announcement of the financier's disappearance made big news, but it did not dismay his investors; their faith was utterly fantastic. One man told a reporter, "If Miller wants $500 from me on Monday, he can have it."

Miller's mother, an honest woman who proved that a mother's devotion is thicker than common sense, sobbed and said, "This is a terrible crime on the part of the newspapers and the police. They have driven my son away."

The flight touched off a belated full-scale investigation. The Floyd Street counting house was padlocked and its ledgers examined. Although Miller's bookkeeping had been non-existent, the police soon got an idea of the fantastic sums the Syndicate had been taking in. From mid-October to mid-November alone, it had received $648,000. After paying out $216,000 in interest, it had pocketed $432,000 in that one-month period.

With Miller out of the way in Montreal, Colonel Ammon adopted the injured air of a lawyer whose client had run out on him. Meanwhile, he gathered up $65,000 more in bonds that Miller owned. The Brooklyn district attorney, suspicious of the shady lawyer, asked him to appear before the Grand Jury. Ammon immediately advised Miller to return, telling him that he would get off lightly if convicted, and be free to spend his money without being hunted as a fugitive. The trusting youth gave himself up.

In April, 1900, he faced a jury. He denied everything, but the jurors needed only five hours, including time for dinner, to convict him. He was sentenced to ten years at hard labor. As he was led off to Grand Central Station for the afternoon train to Sing Sing, Ammon whispered, "Now, Billy, don't go shooting off your mouth up there!"

When reporters asked the cocksure Ammon if he thought Miller would confess now that he had been convicted, he replied, "When I first met Miller I split his upper lip and sewed a button on his lower lip. I have fastened them together securely."

Miller didn't talk, but for an altogether different reason; Ammon was the sole source of support for his family. Every week the lawyer sent five dollars to his wife, who was living with her parents and protesting her husband's innocence, in which she genuinely believed. For a year and a half this went on, with Ammon increasingly confident he was in the clear.

Meanwhile, however, the Brooklyn district attorney quietly continued trying to get Miller to incriminate the lawyer. Soon his task became easier. Miller became seriously ill and spent most of his time in the Sing Sing hospital, first with typhoid fever, then with tuberculosis. He felt he would never leave the prison alive, and his hopes for a financially cheerful future turned to bitterness against Ammon.

In December, 1901, indifferent to the Christmas spirit, the Grand Jury indicted Ammon for receiving stolen funds. The word quickly spread that Miller would testify in return for an eventual pardon, and the word was correct. Ammon was released on his own recognizance, but in June, 1903, when he finally ran out of delaying actions and was called for trial, he came face to face with his former client.

When Miller took the witness stand, spectators were shocked. The swindler, now twenty-six, was almost unrecognizable, with his skin parchmented over cheekbones and his voice so weak that his testimony had to be repeated to the jury. The hand of death seemed hard upon him.

Colonel Ammon, never a quitter, riveted his eyes on the sorry youth and tried to force him to meet his gaze. The prosecutor, aware of Ammon's strength and Miller's weakness, jumped up continually to stand between them.

Miller gave the state the evidence it needed. He testified that the first $30,500 Ammon had banked was stolen money, received from him. He said he had complained to the lawyer of the twenty dollar monthly stipend his wife was receiving, and that Ammon had raised the sum to forty dollars, but only as a loan. Then Miller collapsed and was carried back to jail. Ammon, an old jury-predicter, knew he was done for. He was convicted in a half hour, on the first ballot. Once his fate was decided, he relaxed and chewed tobacco as he stared blandly at the judge, who gave him four-and-a-half-years at hard labor, the maximum term possible under the law.

The saga ran out quickly after that. Ammon was disbarred, served his time, and faded into obscurity. Edward Schlessinger, who had made off with $175,000, gambled and lived high in Paris and Monte Carlo for six years before he died. Miller received his pardon in 1905, after serving half his sentence. He came out broken in health, but probably not broken financially, since all that the authorities ever recovered of an estimated $1,200,000 in loot was $24,000. He did lose his wife, though; she divorced him.

Miller's monumental swindle dropped from most memories as the years passed, but in 1922, a curious incident revived it. When a man was brought into a Long Island court after a fight with his wife, he claimed the whole affair had been his brother-in-law's fault. The brother-in-law, he said, went by the name of William

Schmidt, but was really the notorious 520% Miller, who had been living with him for seventeen years.

Reporters dashed out to Long Island and found Schmidt-Miller, the proprietor of a small country grocery store. They interrupted him as he was explaining to an inquisitive child that he paid one cent for candy sticks and sold them for two cents so he could earn a profit. The reporters asked Miller his opinion of a man who was prominent in the news at the time—Charles Ponzi, the multi-million dollar investment swindler. Miller said he hoped Ponzi would soon be brought to justice; that he had seen through his scheme for a long time just by reading about it in the newspapers.

Miller's comment was given little attention, but it was actually quite revealing. Although Ponzi is generally regarded as having been the most brilliant swindler ever to raid the American wallet, the fact is that he was not even a legitimate phony; he swindled the very idea for his scheme from the workings of the Franklin Syndicate. When Ponzi's immigrant ship entered New York Harbor in 1901, details of Miller's plunder were the talk of the town. And when Ponzi initiated his investment swindle some years later, it was a carbon copy of Miller's.

Few criminals accuse each other of plagiarizing operational plans; nevertheless, the reporters were unimpressed. They got their real story when they left Miller, nosed around the little Long Island town, and asked people what they thought of their once notorious grocer. The newsmen found that no one ever called 520% Miller anything but "Honest Bill."

CHAPTER III

"Goat-Gland" Brinkley

A T EIGHT P.M. on the drought-dry night of April 1, 1930, the rural people of Kansas clamped headphones over their ears and tuned in the Milford station, KFKB—"Kansas First, Kansas Best." They were just in time.

"Now, folks, friends, and all who are weary and oppressed," they heard the announcer say, "Doctor John R. Brinkley will deliver his message to humanity, with love for all in his heart."

It was only radio, so the weary and oppressed couldn't see John Romulus Brinkley, a small, dapper man with a bobbing, bullet head, a gray goatee, and hands heavy with diamonds. But, at 1050 on their dials, they could hear his peculiarly captivating monotone.

My dear, dear friends—my patients, my supplicants. Your many letters lie here before me, touching testimonials of your pain, your grief, and the wretchedness that is visited upon the innocent. I can reply now to a few—just a few. Others I shall answer by mail.

But, oh my friends, you must help me—remember that your letters asking advice must be accompanied by two dollars, which barely covers the cost of postage, stenographic hire, and office rent. I am your friend, but not even a great baron of Wall Street could withstand the ruinous cost of helping you unless this small fee accompanies your letter.

That was John Brinkley, better known to millions of chuckling Americans in the 1920's and '30's as "Goat-Gland" Brinkley. He was the obsessed, swindling megalomaniac who offered to make old men young again by endowing them with the sex glands of billy goats, at $750 a pair—$1,500 if the glands of a very young goat were used.

To this day, there is not the wispiest evidence that any animal's glands can rejuvenate a man sexually, but the search for the fountain of lost youth is desperate and dogged. Aware of this ageless truth, Brinkley operated on many a bank account. In sixteen years he gave 5,000 pairs of goat glands to men from half the states in the Union, then sent them home to their impatient wives. When he finally rolled up his medical degree, which had been ground out by a diploma mill, the "goat man" had earned several million dollars and the epithet of "the greatest charlatan in medical history."

Still, there have been many charlatans, and "greatest" is an abused word. What distinguished Brinkley—and sometimes made his antics humorous—was his rubbery ability to bounce back from a battery of knockout punches. Politicians, foreign officials, leaders of the American Medical Association, and Herbert Hoover's vice-president stayed awake nights wondering how to cope with him. He even frightened the Democratic and Republican parties, by running for governor of Kansas. Everybody who was politically anybody admitted that the reason

Brinkley didn't enter the State House was because of the way the votes were counted—or, rather, weren't counted.

All in all, John Romulus Brinkley was a genuine American phenomenon, a demagogue with a Jimmy Valentine finger on the pulse of the people.

For a long while during his amazing career, Brinkley was tight-lipped about his boyhood days and probably for a good reason. He was not stupid and must have understood, in those moments of painful honesty no man can ever completely evade, that the seeds of his rascality were sown before he was old enough to whistle.

Brinkley was born in 1885, in hilly Beta, North Carolina, a money-parched town of two hundred farmers fenced off from the world by the Great Smokies and the Blue Ridge. He didn't get a recognizable word past his lips until he was three, a tardiness that mortified his stern, hard-bitten mother. Candace Brinkley was determined to make the boy speak, and thrashed him by the clock.

Father Brinkley was a dreamer and often told the boy why he had given him the middle name of Romulus. It was the name of the legendary son of Mars, who was thrown into the Tiber and rescued and suckled by a wolf. "Romulus was made a god by the Romans," the old man said, "and you will be great, too."

Tuberculosis killed Candace Brinkley before young John was six and his father died when he was ten. The boy was left with an impoverished aunt and a head full of escapist daydreams. Slumped in Beta's one-room dilapidation of a grade school, he cast himself in Messianic roles.

"I thought of John Brinkley freeing the slaves," he said later, "John Brinkley illuminating the world, John Brinkley facing an assassin's bullet for the sake of his people, John Brinkley healing the sick . . ."

By the time he was sixteen, his glory-bound mind had outgrown tobacco-picking Beta, where it was a rare man who saw $200 cash money over a year's time. He tried to escape the life of a mule follower by carrying the mail down the mountain to the Southern Railway station in nearby Sylva. But even Sylva bored him. So he made his way up to Baltimore, where he told the dean of the Johns Hopkins Medical School that he wanted to become a doctor.

The dean chatted, led the boy over a few basic educational hurdles, and found him wanting. Brinkley interpreted the interview somewhat differently and claimed Johns Hopkins wouldn't share its knowledge with him "because I didn't own a pair of shoes."

Either way, Baltimore was not completely luckless. Leaving the grounds of Johns Hopkins, the shoeless one was buttonholed by a man who operated a "private" medical school. He heard the boy's story and assured him that university snobbishness need be no bar to an earnest young fellow. After signing up for a pay-as-you-go correspondence course, Brinkley left for New York with an armful of herb-doctor books that prescribed sassafras tea to cool the blood.

Now he could hardly wait to hang out his shingle. Back in Sylva, a railroad agent had taught him how to handle a telegraph key; in New York, he spent impatient days tapping out Western Union telegrams and perplexed nights mastering his book learning. Four years later, he was told by several doctors that herb medicine was on the way out.

Disgusted, he packed up and returned to the mountain country, where he met and married a Daisy Mae type of hill girl named Sally Wike. Together they went off to Chicago, where she persuaded him to enroll in another herb-worshipping institution, Bennett Medical College. This time, Western Union used him on the night shift. When he finished his studies, he was awarded a diploma, for some strange reason, from an outfit called the Eclectic Medical University of Kansas City.

With his formidable parchment, Brinkley returned to New York where, as they were fond of saying even fifty years ago, all the money was. He wangled a permit to practice, and set up an herb shop. But, restless healer that he was, he became bored after only two years. It was then that he met a man who said he knew where the *real* money was.

In Greenville, South Carolina, the pair set themselves up in a rambling old house as "electromedic specialists." Again Brinkley found the world unready. Even in South Carolina, home of one of the lowest literacy rates in the nation, people read enough to sense that "electromedics" was either ahead of its time or timely quackery.

Brinkley soon broke with his partner and headed for Fulton, Kansas. He picked up medical licenses from Arkansas and Tennessee; in those days these were good enough for Kansas. Organized medicine was that disorganized.

While Brinkley was having these professional ups and downs, his personal life was even more hectic. Once she got to know the man, pretty Sally Wike couldn't stand him. She asked for a divorce but he said no. In April, 1910, she left him, taking their baby daughter and his Western

Union paycheck. He found her in August, made off with the baby, and went to Canada, refusing to return until she dropped her humiliating divorce action.

They were reunited, but a year later Sally left once more while eight months pregnant. Broke and desperate, she returned with their second child. But the following year, when she celebrated the birth of their third daughter by disappearing again, Brinkley swallowed his ego and gave her a divorce.

That summer, while visiting in Memphis, he met a doctor's daughter and married her before the leaves fell. Minnie Telitha Jones was her name; she was a sturdy girl who, if nothing else, could stand John Brinkley. She was not even dismayed when, shortly after their marriage, he was arrested on a bad check charge. He beat the charge, and the couple beat it to Kansas together.

Fulton, Kansas, small as it was, held the beginnings of big things. People who remember Brinkley's political prancing do not generally know it was in Fulton that the voters first discovered his charm. He and Minnie were in town less than six months when he was elected mayor, no less. He served for a year, while tending patients on the side.

His clients were awed. He had begun to cultivate a goatee and they were further impressed by the dexterousness of his oddly pale-skinned hands. A rapidly receding hairline gave him a broad forehead, and a smile played constantly over his owlish face. With his goatee and his strangely beguiling voice, he appeared more a visiting specialist from Vienna than a visiting fireman from the Carolina hills.

But Brinkley was not taken in by this one-horse success. Knowing that Fulton was only a way point toward the financial peaks, he spent his evenings researching the medical facilities of other Kansas towns. By the time his mayoralty term expired, he had settled on Milford, a rutroaded prairie town close to the Nebraska border, that had neither a doctor nor a hospital. And so Minnie and the Mayor said fond farewell to Fulton and disappeared into the setting sun. On October 7, 1917, they entered fateful Milford, where Brinkley was to make famous his lip-smacking approach to sexual rejuvenation.

Everyone who later investigated Brinkley agrees that he opened a drug store immediately, but the reports of how he opened his surgical career differ drastically.

According to Brinkley, he was grinding away with his mortar and pestle one afternoon when a farmer dropped in and cracker-barreled about his sad home life. "Claimed he'd been sexually dead for sixteen years," said Brinkley, who always preferred the vernacular to the stuffiness of medical terminology. The farmer led the conversation around to goat glands and finally suggested that Brinkley give him a pair. The good doctor demurred, partly because he wasn't sure transplantation was the road to rejuvenation, partly because he didn't have a goat. The man solved that by assuming all responsibility and scaring up a goat. Brinkley operated and reported that "happy results were obtained."

A year later, he announced, he delivered his patient's wife of a strapping baby boy, whom the exuberant man insisted on naming Billy, in tribute to the goat.

So much for Brinkley's version, which is not to accuse it of being stodgy; his explanations rarely were. But another version of the origin of his use of goat glands is no less engrossing. It holds that during his studious evenings in Fulton, he had become intrigued by rejuvenation work being carried on in Paris by a Russian named Serge Voronoff.

Actually Voronoff was a serious experimenter who confined his work to animals and performed fifty-two testicular grafting operations on chimpanzess. He made few claims but his work generated tremendous interest, as well as derision from those who felt he was intruding into untouchable facets of life.

Another rejuvenation investigator, Dr. Eugen Steinach of Vienna—whose reports were also on Brinkley's reading list—abandoned the fountain of youth field with bitterness when he was also condemned for "tampering with sex." "If I had dealt with the physiological structure of the left wing of the grasshopper," he said, "my efforts would have been highly appreciated."

Brinkley understood that few grasshoppers or chimps were worth much money, so he decided to rejuvenate humans. Within a year after delivering Billy boy, he gave goat glands to a cousin and to a bank teller who, shortly afterward, was released from a mental institution. Brinkley claimed the man had recovered both his virility and his marbles.

The word got around and soon Brinkley was a big name in northern Kansas. Although he had changed his middle name to Richard, he still recalled Father Brinkley's story of his original namesake. "You will be great, too," were the words he quoted to worshipful Minnie. He told her of his boyhood daydreams of facing the assassin's bullet, which thrilled her, and about his fantasy of John Brinkley healing the sick, which she thought was more practical.

He saw the practicalities, too. In August, 1918, with money from his lucrative practice, the healer established a fifty-bed hospital that bore his name. This provided the first of scores of opportunities he would find to have his name engraved in huge letters. It was an impressive hospital, with rooms for nurses and surgical assistants, dozens of trays of gleaming knives, and naturally, storage facilities for goat glands.

The hospital did not come any too soon, for once the wives of his original customers promulgated the doctrine that their husbands were making them happy again, the crush was on, in ages up to eighty; few stopped to consider how strong the power of suggestion must have been on men whose virility had been lagging.

Brinkley wanted to oblige, but he faced a serious problem. It *was* serious; there weren't enough goats in Kansas! But the goat-man demonstrated that he was equal to the crisis. He knew that whatever commodities the fair and nearby state of Arkansas might lack, goats were not among them. By the opening of 1920, Brinkley agents were swarming from Texarkana to the outskirts of Memphis, buying, renting, and kidnaping goats. Arkansas swarmed with nannie widows.

On the premise that high costs demand high fees, Brinkley set $750 as the price for transplanting a pair of goat glands. But one day he saw even greater possibilities when a middle-aged Texas oilman flew up to Milford, checked into the Brinkley Hospital, and sat down to discuss his problem.

"Doc," he said, "you can't fool me. There's no way old goats can make a fellow young again."

Brinkley was startled at this querulousness and prepared to usher the oilman out. But the man wouldn't budge.

"You know as well as I do," he said furtively, "that the only goats that'll do the trick is young billies—not more'n a year old. You won't get a penny one until you show me a no-foolin' *young* billy!" He tweaked Brinkley's beard and grinned.

Brinkley grinned back. "Didn't know they grew fellows so smart down in Texas." His washed-blue eyes measured the situation carefully, for he realized he was nearing a new lode of opportunity. "Now I'll tell you what. I'll give you a year-old billy, but it'll cost you. That's a $1,500 job."

"Doc," the Texan said, "I didn't fly up here to argue about numbers. You get the billy."

Brinkley got the billy and the oilman got the no-foolin' glands.

Milford had never seen such action. Merchants beamed as the rail station clogged. Fifty men arrived for appointments every Monday morning; forty were handled by a half-dozen surgical assistants and the great man himself shifted ten sets of reproductive glands from goats to men. The patients were then put to bed, where they rested until Friday, when they were shooed out to make room for the next contingent. Each Monday morning Brinkley greeted the fresh hopefuls by remarking that their predecessors went home "scratching and kicking."

Money poured in and a brand new railroad spur delivered Arkansas goats by the carload. Brinkley built neat cottages for his assistant transplanters and a dormitory for his nurses, and gave Milford a modern water supply system.

He even organized a baseball team and named it the Brinkley Goats.

But that old devil restlessness would not be stilled. The goat-man suspected that the $15,000 he was clearing each week was like the Republican River that meandered past the town. "A nice river," he would say, "but it's not the Mississippi, is it?"

Which accounts, in late 1922, for his placing a call to an advertising man in Kansas City. The adman came over to Milford and an earnest consultation followed. Patent-medicine houses and pseudo-doctors were getting away with murder in their newspaper advertisements, but Brinkley wanted to go them one better. He was looking for the biggest huckster horn that money could buy.

That's what he got. The adman suggested he pioneer in the newfangled field of radio. Thousands were buying sets just to hear Paul Whiteman, the King of Jazz. People spent entire evenings having their ears filled with sound. Why not give them the inimitable sound of John Brinkley?

And so he did. In Milford, he erected KFKB, a station so powerful it carried into Nebraska, Missouri, and Oklahoma. With a license from the old Federal Radio Commission, KFKB took to the air fifteen and one-half hours a day, acquainting the folks with the wonders and troubles of the prostate gland and supplying cornball music and yodelers for interludes. Sensing the power of repetition that is so irritatingly employed today, he drummed it into his listeners that "a man is as old as his glands."

While he knew he had a good thing, he didn't realize the amazing power that radio held. Letters poured in from bedeviled people, curious about the goat gland operations they had heard extolled. He referred them to the Brinkley Hospital; it was the least he could do.

Then, with no one else's help, he fetched up the brainstorm of the 1920's. He decided that people must have a lot of troubles besides sexual ones and so he went into the business of general diagnosis and prescription by air. He rehearsed little medical homilies before his adoring Minnie, and if poor dead Mother Brinkley could have heard him, she would have had to agree that young John sure had learned to talk:

Now here is a letter from a dear mother—a dear little mother who holds to her breast a babe of nine months. She should take No. 2 and—yes, No. 17—and she will be helped. Brinkley's 2 and 17. She should order them from the Milford Drug Company, Milford, Kansas, and they shall be sent to you, Mother—collect. May the Lord guard and protect you, Mother. The postage will be prepaid.

What did Brinkley's 2 and 17 consist of? A secret formula, perhaps? A new drug? A premature tranquilizer? No, John Brinkley's imagination was more down to earth. One was an aspirin compound and the other was castor oil, both labeled with numbers instead of names.

In the seven years that followed 1923, Brinkley's "Medical Question Box" diagnosed everything from fallen arches to cancer. On one broadcast alone, he diagnosed fortyfour different complaints, in each case prescribing from one to ten of his numbers game medicinals. He gathered up lists of thousands of names, hawked his wares through the mails, and hired fifty girls to open the returns. It was not unusual for 50,000 letters to arrive every day in Milford, and soon, a new post office had to be built; it was bigger than all those in the surrounding area combined.

The goat-man's personal tastes turned *nouveau riche*. He bought a cabin plane, big enough to hold a desk and secretaries, with which he could fly his message of hope around the Midwest. Then he bought a $7,000 Lincoln and three other cars, including a sixteen-cylinder red Cadillac on which the name John Brinkley was engraved in thirteen places. He picked up two yachts, one a 170-footer that had belonged to movie magnate Joe Schenck, and named them—what else?—the John Brinkley I and II. (When Minnie bore a son they named *him* John Brinkley III.) Brinkley's tailored suits were ordered ten at a time, his cravat held a diamond stickpin, and he became a two-fisted wearer of 12-carat diamond rings.

But life during this period was not all Cadillacs and encrusted cravats for Brinkley.

In 1924 he was called to Los Angeles by Harry Chandler, a prominent newspaper publisher, who offered him $40,000 to rejuvenate several aging employees. The California Medical Board granted him a thirty-day permit, under which he performed his surgery, but no sooner did he get out of the state than a ruckus occurred. The American Medical Association offered evidence of his shoddy education and charged that he had bought his medical diploma. Brinkley, who was back in Milford, was indicted for violation of medical practice laws and California's attorney general asked Governor Jonathan M. Davis of Kansas to return him for trial.

But Brinkley was a popular Sunflower by then, and Governor Davis retorted, "We're going to keep John Brinkley here as long as he lives!" The Governor further indicated his confidence by reaching into a musty statute book and appointing the goat-man an admiral in Kansas' landlocked navy. Brinkley erupted in a stunning blue uniform with "scrambled eggs" and vice-admiral's stripes.

The unorthodox practitioner also had problems with his mumbo jumbo drugs. The potions were taking business away from the patent medicine houses and also from those kindly corner drug store men whom we have always been taught to honor along with our mothers and our flag. If everybody bought by the number from Brinkley—well, it was downright unpatriotic.

So one day he received a delegation of pill-rollers who stated their economic case angrily. They might raise some legal hell, they warned. On the spot, Brinkley formed the Brinkley Pharmaceutical Association, an aggregation of druggists who would carry his privately numbered compounds. In return for the windfall, they would kick back a percentage. Soon 500 druggists were willing to do just that. In one three month period, the kickbacks came to $27,856. So the tenor of the KFKB broadcasts changed. Now the citizens heard:

This little lady has been seeing spots before her eyes, has dizzy spells, and is constipated. Prescriptions 66 and 74, which she can procure at the Acme Drugstore in —————, at five dollars and seven dollars, will bring her relief.

That was much better for all concerned, with the exception of sick people. The druggists were less principled, but more cheerful, and the outlets for the drugs were less restricted and more profitable. Financial matters galloped along so well that Brinkley opened his own Bank of Milford.

This backscratching arrangement built a powerful wall around the goat-man's operations, but it also hastened the day when he would have to face strong opposition. For, while local doctors might have been content to ignore him in matters of rejuvenation, the good gray medical profession could not afford to ignore his radio diagnosis of disease.

The fact was that the profession was just then beginning to become good and gray. It had been only twenty years since the Rockefeller-financed Flexner investigation exposed a huge number of doctors and medical educators as well-meaning incompetents or ill-motivated charlatans. Only nine years had passed since the diploma-mill scandals had closed down the herb-school parchment printers. So, while doctors fretted over the idea of diagnosing patients without ever seeing them, all they could do was write rednecked letters to the AMA. And the AMA's machine was a Model T compared to its powerhouse of today.

Finally, in 1929, the Kansas City *Star* (a Missouri paper, but influential in Kansas) started looking for a way to keelhaul Brinkley. A. B. MacDonald, a crack reporter, nosed around Milford, visited Brinkley letter writers and patients, retraced the rejuvenator's trail to California and back, and dug deeply into his remote past. In 1930, the ink flowed and the *Star* accused Brinkley of everything this side of murder.

It went back to his acquisition of a Kansas medical license and charged fraud. He had used his diploma-mill degree to obtain a license from the Connecticut Eclectic Board, which in turn got him licenses from Arkansas and Tennessee, which had reciprocity with Connecticut. Kansas had reciprocity with Arkansas and Tennessee and so, the *Star* said, Brinkley had entered Kansas medicine through a rathole. Then it showed that a 1923 investiga-

tion had exposed the Connecticut Eclectic Board and revoked 167 of its licenses, including Brinkley's. So, the
paper said, he had no right to practice in Kansas under
any circumstances.

Then it was revealed that the goat-man had pleaded
guilty during Prohibition in 1920 to selling alcohol. That
didn't hit very hard, but another charge did. The *Star*
found and interviewed Sally Wike, Brinkley's first wife,
and reviewed their spattered marital life. It alleged that
Sally had never left him, but had been driven out each
time, and was finally deserted with her three children.

And finally, the paper came close to charging "the
Brinkley industry" with outright murder. It said that a
New Jersey carpenter died of tetanus after submitting to a
goat gland operation.

To top the revelations, the *Star* printed interviews with
Brinkley patients who said that, after the psychological
uplift of their operations had let down, they were still as
old as their original glands.

The cumulative effect of the exposé was devastating. As
Brinkley read each day's blast, his goatee jiggled and his
lips moved in excitement. He read passages to Minnie, who
wept at the travail a medical pioneer had to suffer.

"John," she said on recovering her practicality, "what
if people believe those lies? What will happen to your
practice?"

"Darling," Brinkley said, "I've learned a lot from goats.
Did you ever see a billy butt?"

He hustled up a lawyer and filed a libel suit against the
Star for $5,000,000. Then he went down to KFKB,
grasped the microphone firmly, and complained to the
people. He said that poor boys who try to get into exclu-

sive clubs—such as medicine—were always persecuted. He had never been one of the clique and never would be. And anyway, he said, the crux of the matter was that his non-commercial KFKB was luring listeners from the *Star's* own WDAF, which was costing the station advertising revenue. That, he said, was what bothered the Kansas City *Star.*

Letters of support and encouragement poured in and there was no noticeable letup of patients who got off the train at Milford. It was 1930, the depression was on, and bitter people were inclined to give underdogs the benefit of the doubt over entrenched authorities.

Brinkley relaxed and continued talking and transplanting, meanwhile purchasing another airplane. But in April he received an order to appear before the Kansas Board of Medical Examiners and show cause why his license to practice should not be revoked. The AMA was charging him with fraud, misrepresentation, gross immorality, and a black satchel of other misdeeds.

Three weeks later a right cross came from Washington. The Federal Radio Commission notified him of a hearing that would determine whether his KFKB license should be renewed. The pressure had been turned on.

If Brinkley was concerned by these one-two blows, he didn't show it. While his assistants continued operating at the Brinkley Hospital, he conferred with attorneys and lined up witnesses. When the medical board hearing opened on July 15, in Topeka's Hotel Kansan, he was ready to steal the show.

A colorful Kansas historian, W. G. Clugston, explained how he did it, in his book *Rascals in Democracy*:

He called upon his satisfied customers to come in and testify for him—and they came like clansmen called from the hills to do battle against a great enemy. They came from all walks of life . . . butchers and bankers, farmers and railroad men, traveling salesmen and coal miners; there were wives of men who had submitted to the operations; there was a regular medical doctor from Illinois and an irregular practitioner from Missouri—they all came to declare under oath that his operations really produced rejuvenating effects.

Day after day the papers had to report what seemed to be vindicating testimony. Brinkley sat at the defense table stroking his goatee and smoking aromatic Murads. He said he would keep witnesses coming all summer. When the medical board shut off the deluge, he put 500 affidavits into the record. Then he challenged the doctors to observe one of his goat gland operations. It was difficult to convict a man without doing that, so they traveled to Milford and sat in the operating room while Brinkley performed. They agreed he was skillful.

But the goat-man really couldn't win this round. The bolo punch was delivered near the close of the hearing in mid-August, after the introduction of medical testimony that excluded any possibility of rejuvenation by goats. Suddenly Brinkley was confronted with an exhibit there was no combating. It consisted of certificates bearing the names of forty-two of his patients. They were death certificates; he had had to sign them because the patients, under his care, had died.

In September his Kansas license was revoked. He said the plot against him had been engineered by the AMA, which he called "a meat cutters' union," but that he was prepared. He quickly hired regularly licensed surgeons to operate for him and got ready to fight in

Washington, D. C., for the retention of his radio license.

There, the hearing was no less bumptious. Brinkley took the stand and told how he had given new life to the seven Los Angeles newspapermen when *Star* reporter MacDonald leaped to his feet and shouted, "Yes, except that one died!"

That hurt. And so did evidence that he had repeatedly violated good taste. The transcript of his April 1, 1930 program provided an example. It told of his randy reply to an Olathe woman who had complained she was having too many children.

"I suggest you have your husband sterilized," Brinkley had told her in his most lecherous voice, "and then you will be safe, providing you don't get out in anybody else's cow pasture and get in with some other bull."

The Commissioners were shocked. They refused to renew KFKB's license, but only by a three to two vote. Brinkley won the right to continue broadcasting while he appealed.

Smiling to reporters on the way to the Washington Airport, he promised he would not deprive them of a good story by giving up. He and Minnie flew down to Florida to rest from their battles. There he lay in the sun and read that the Kansas Supreme Court had upheld revocation of his license and said he had organized charlatanism to prey on human weakness, ignorance, and credulity. Quietly, he had his libel suit against the Kansas City *Star* dismissed and paid the court costs.

Brinkley appeared to have been knocked out, but the practical fact was that up to the moment at least, he was untouched. He could still broadcast and his hired doctors could still operate and collect for him. Furthermore, his clubbed but unbowed head was still capable of strange fertility. As a matter of fact, on the Florida sand it spawned one of the strangest sagas of modern American politics. He rose, took Minnie by the arm, and flew back to Kansas to hatch it.

"John R. Brinkley will be the next governor of Kansas!" he announced on his arrival in Milford. It was late September, 1930.

His secretary gasped, screamed with delight, and called the newspapers in Kansas City and Topeka. Hours later, the whole nation knew that the medicine man of Milford was running for governor of Kansas.

From the days of the Populist political uprising of the 1890's—when Kansans were urged to "Raise less corn and more hell!"—the state had been a romping ground for political mavericks, but never had a candidate run on a goat gland platform! Reporters descended on Milford for a Roman holiday. Armed by the chuckling politicians of Topeka, they sprang a critical piece of news at Brinkley's first press conference.

"Doctor Brinkley, do you know the election laws of this state?"

"You are referring to the final dates on which candidates may file?" Brinkley asked.

Yes, they were.

"I am aware that it is too late for my name to appear on the ballots. The people of Kansas will write in the name of John R. Brinkley, and I will see you in Topeka."

For the politicians and the press, that removed any semblance of seriousness from the affair. No man could expect almost a quarter of a million people to write his name in—and that's how many he would need to win. Besides, his supporters would be crackpot illiterates. The Republicans went on campaigning for Frank Haucke and the Democrats banged away for Harry Woodring. They only referred to Brinkley for laughs.

Which just proves once again that politicians must never 1) overlook the holes in their own armor or 2) underestimate the power of a demagogue.

The problem was that the regular candidates were no world beaters to start with. When the Kansas City *Star* published their personality sketches, William Allen White, the celebrated Emporia *Gazette* editor, was moved to say that Haucke looked like a "sissy," Woodring like a "sap."

Those were the armor chinks, and to them Brinkley brought a bunker of opportunism. He was aware of the discontent the depression had spread through the nation. In Kansas, where the drought was emasculating farmland and wheat was down to sixty cents a bushel and still sliding, the farmers were looking for a man on a white mule. Brinkley had no mule, but he had a fast airplane and a bellowing radio station. Over KFKB, from dawn to past dusk and in several languages, the appeal went out. He said "Clean out, clean up, and keep Kansas clean!"—a time-tested slogan—and he told how things would change in November.

"If I am elected," he promised, "I will build a lake in every county in Kansas. The water will be evaporated and pour down as gentle rain on the fertile fields." He offered so much over KFKB that John Gunther later called him "the first American demagogue to use radio for political purposes in a big way."

Then he flew up, down, and across the state, neglecting

no area, pledging old-age pensions, state-financed game preserves, and, above all, lower taxes. Soon he was speaking to 10,000 people at a time, holding giant torchlight rallies, at which they learned to spell his name correctly by shouting its letters in unison: J-O-H-N R. B-R-I-N-K-L-E-Y. It was a rousing orgy of the oppressed, salaaming to their savior. The savior passed out pencils and sample ballots and sent the oppressed home to practice.

At the end of the campaign, when Brinkley was teaching spelling to 20,000 voters a rally, the politicians finally became nervous and decided to man the polling places in force. Their apprehension was well grounded, as early returns showed in the Wichita *Beacon* of November 4:

BRINKLEY SWEEPING WICHITA

Milford Candidate is 2 to 1
Over Haucke

Woodring Runs Third

But that was premature. As election night wore on and the politicians' faces grew longer, the order went out from Topeka to cancel every write-in on which even an *i* hadn't been dotted. That was legal, and ballots went out every window, but the next morning Brinkley had still scared their pants off. The totals read: Woodring: 217,171; Haucke: 216,920; Brinkley: 183,278.

Brinkley claimed he'd been euchered out of 56,000 votes and had really won, but he couldn't get anyone in authority to listen. Haucke, who'd lost by 251 votes, purred like a kitten. *Nobody* wanted a recount, out of which Goat-Gland Brinkley might well emerge as governor. Why, the man had been credited with 30,000 more votes than

William Allen White got while *on* the ballolt in 1924. He had even received 20,000 write-ins and won three counties in Oklahoma!

Minnie Brinkley cried, but the goat-man was stoically philosophic. He realized the remarkable thing he had accomplished and it was savor enough for the moment. After all, 1932, another election year, was just around the corner. And didn't he have a plan up his sleeve that would keep his voice hammering at the inner ear of his fellow citizens?

He certainly did. In between his political gyrations, he had sized up the radio situation down in sunny Mexico. Mexican officials were miffed because Canada and the United States had already taken over the best air channels on the continent. So they were not inclined to worry about the niceties of licensing a radio station on a channel already in use north of the border.

Brinkley lined up a permit for a $350,000 border-blaster, a 100,000-watt station that was being built for him in a scratchy hamlet just over the Rio Grande from Del Rio, Texas. In June, 1931, he sold KFKB to a Wichita insurance company for $90,000 and went on the air over XER, Villa Acuna, with an engaging slogan: "Sunshine Between the Nations." And he didn't have to leave Milford to do it, either. His broadcasts were recorded, at a monthly cost of $10,000. A pittance.

As the French say, the more things change, the more they remain the same. Goat gland operations continued in Milford, at $750 to $1,500 apiece, people were still being told their lost youth was hiding in a billy goat, and John R. Brinkley was still applying the numbers game to every human ailment from gallstones to hangnail.

Not only that, but he went wild over XER. After Senor Martinez and the Dwarfie Boys finished their songs, he came on and put the needle to the orthodox medical profession. "Don't let your doctor two-dollar you to death," he said. "Come to the Brinkley Hospital." On the side, XER peddled fortunetelling, gold mine stocks, horoscopes, and oil burners. His advertising rates were $1,700 an hour.

XER was easily the most powerful radio station in the world at the time. It boomed a wide swath up the Mississippi Valley to the Canadian border and was heard clearly east to Florida. In fact, Brinkley had to reduce his operating wattage when Del Rio residents picked up their telephones and got him for fifteen minutes on his favorite subject, the cause and cure of prostate gland troubles. Some people said Mexico was crazy to let him carry on like that, but Mexico took care of its own. Behind XER the government had erected giant steel towers; to hear Brinkley, Mexicans had to live in the United States.

And in the United States, Kansans received big news loud and clear; Brinkley had filed as an independent candidate for governor. On the 1932 ballot, his name would appear with those of Democratic incumbent Woodring and a Republican oilman, Alf Landon.

Since he was recording his broadcasts, the goat-man was free to roam the state, where wheat was now down to thirty-two cents a bushel. He toured every county seat and hundreds of smaller communities. In Dodge City he drew bigger crowds than Democratic and Republican rallies combined, and at Liberal, Coldwater, and Salina he made promises even more extravagant than he had in 1930. Speaking from a sound truck bathed in the glow of a spotlight, he used his soothsayer's monotone and pledged he would pave thousands of miles of roads, distribute schoolbooks free, and reduce the minimum cost of license plates from six and one-half dollars to two and one-half dollars.

Alf Landon retorted that such a reduction was ridiculously modest; he would bring the minimum down to sixty cents. The politicians were in a stew. When Brinkley left a huge rally at Emporia, the correspondent of *The Nation* wrote: "All signs in Kansas point to the election this year of Dr. John R. Brinkley. . . . The farmers seem to be almost solidly behind him."

Brinkley ignored the fact that a Democrat was running against him and, to its embarrassment, contributed money to the national Democratic Party.

In Emporia, the fur flew. When the folks in huge Soden's Grove burst into Brinkley's campaign song, "He's the Man!" their voices were heard down the street at the *Gazette's* offices by the editor, William Allen White, who blew a gasket. He called seven Kansas editors and publishers together to map a coordinated anti-Brinkley campaign, then knocked out a sod-busting editorial titled, "Save Kansas!"

"Are we going to bow our heads after the election?" White asked. "Bow in shame that the intelligent, patriotic people of this state didn't have the sense or the courage to avert this disgrace? Shall Kansas be greeted by a gibing ba-a-a, the cry of the billy goat, when they walk the streets of other states?"

White raised so much anti-Brinkley hell that the New York *Times* cautioned him against being so vitriolic. "There is a perversity in human nature," the *Times* quipped, "that sometimes prefers the goats to the sheep."

White responded by telling the voters darkly that Brinkley had spent over $200,000 already and that insidious forces must be at work behind him. "Do they think that by making grass widows out of nannie goats this man can make all this money to spend as lavishly as it is going these days?" he asked.

Brinkley, cheered by the publicity, sent the *Gazette* a crated billy goat that sat in its offices through a hot summer afternoon until White could prevail on a small boy to take it home as a pet. In a dither, he wrote: "The Kansas fray never was so fraptious, so entirely galluptious as the fray we are now fraying in this old state."

It had to be said that, for all his faults, dullness was never a Brinkley failing. Two weeks before election day he learned that the State Department, more out of national embarrassment than partisan pique, was pressuring the Mexican government to shut down XER. Interrupting his campaign, he flew to Washington and sat down with a fellow Kansan, Vice-President Charles Curtis. He asked Curtis to assure him a fair deal and got a vague response. So he laid it on the line. If XER was closed, he would seek the Republican Presidential nomination in 1936. Curtis, sensitive to the vagaries of Kansas politics and to blackmail, hurried him over to the State Department. The pressure on the Mexicans halted.

Brinkley flew back to Kansas and wound up his campaign with a town-hopping tour of the Corn Belt. On election eve, he telephoned a victory speech down to Villa Acuna and retired, prepared to awaken as the Messiah of Kansas.

It was not to be. He swept the rural vote, but he couldn't trump the big-city boys and their newspapers. The final vote stood: Landon: 278,581; Woodring: 272,944; Brinkley: 244,607.

Landon was reelected in 1934 and became the GOP presidential candidate in 1936. Woodring, beaten by votes that Brinkley attracted despite the Democratic national landslide, was consoled with the secretary of war post in the New Deal cabinet. And Brinkley, the maverick goat-man, said the hell with Kansas. He closed up the Milford hospital and moved to Del Rio, where he established a new clinic in a hotel.

Politically, the defeat was severe. But Brinkley could at least find solace in money, and XER was raking it in. He built a $200,000 marble and tile home on six acres and had his name installed in neon over a swimming pool and splashing fountains. He soaked in the pool on sunny afternoons and looked across the International Line to the towers of XER. And he backed up his cash assets with 7,000 acres in North Carolina, an oil well, three airplanes, twelve automobiles, and a cluster of south Texas citrus groves.

In Del Rio, he was warmly regarded by the leading merchants, who appreciated the business he attracted. They made him president of the Rotary Club.

Del Rio quickly became the new Mecca of rejuvenation, and another shifty surgeon opened up shop as a competitor. That was a free-for-all the goat-man liked. He sent representatives down to the railroad station, where they engaged his competitor's agents in hand-to-hand combat. Like European hotel porters at boat dock, each side tried to shag patients to its employer. Brinkley's men lost few customers.

At the hospital the patients were greeted by a front-office man who informed them that recapture of youth was a cash proposition. He was equipped with legal documents necessary to secure liens on mortgages, convert securities into cash, and otherwise insure that no patient left in debt to Brinkley.

Nearing fifty now, the great man felt it was time these worldly efforts were engraved for posterity. He hired a writer to listen to him by the hour and set down his exploits. Never was a paranoid's self-infatuation so faithfully recorded between hard covers. The writer amassed 75,000 usable words by employing as many rapturous adjectives as Brinkley had used scalpels. Brinkley was so grateful he peddled the book over XER.

Then the medicine man made a historic decision. He was abandoning goat gland operations because, he announced, he had found an even shorter route to virility. This consisted of injections of mercurochrome combined with a duct tieing operation; cost: $750, plus $100 for five postoperative ampules to be injected by a local physician at home. The ampules were found, on analysis, to contain one part bluing to 100,000 parts water.

Brinkley was so happy with his new formula that he made the first serious blunder of his charmed career; he didn't see the handwriting that suddenly appeared on the wall. Mexico finally decided to silence the border-blasters. In February, 1934, the government announced suspension of XER's license for breaking every law that regulated medical advertising.

Brinkley sped over to Villa Acuna and confirmed his suspicion that he was regarded as a sort of north-of-the-border god. The government had better not tamper with their State of Coahuila, the locals said. Faithful Minnie tried to insure that the government wouldn't interfere by hurrying down to Mexico City with cash in unmarked bills. But it was no go. The government sent a radio inspector to Villa Acuna to take over. When the villagers threatened to lynch him, he retreated; but early in March he returned with troops and the citizens subsided.

Brinkley stood at the edge of his estate and watched the take-over through binoculars. He knew the jig was up and announced he was closing XER to "prevent civil war between the Mexican Government and Coahuila."

That was the first blow from which he didn't bounce. The second came after an ill-advised decision to try once more for the governorship of Kansas. He filed for the Republican nomination, but Alf Landon wiped him out in the August, 1934, primary. It was too difficult to accept, but in Kansas his halo was losing its luminescence. Absence makes the memory grow dimmer.

A third deflation came two years later, when he asked the Federal District Court to force Kansas to reinstate his medical license. Robert E. Lewis, one of three judges who heard the case, called him "an out-and-out charlatan." Another judge said his old goat gland operation did "about as much good as putting a piece of dough under the skin."

Hearing of this dictum, the Texas Board of Medical Examiners became aroused, so Brinkley shored up his position by establishing another hospital in Arkansas, on a country club estate that contained a 100-acre lake and was surrounded by a 360-acre golf course. In the heart of nearby Little Rock, he opened the Romulus Drugstore, at which acid-stomach pills were mailed out at five dollars for a hundred and a laxative at three dollars for six ounces. Orders for these items soared at one point to 2,000 letters a day. Brinkley hardly had time to count the money, he was so busy commuting by plane between Little Rock and Del Rio.

But he could not forever evade the inevitable. The end was clearly signaled when Dr. Morris Fishbein, editor of the AMA magazine, *Hygeia*, called him a charlatan and quack in print. Brinkley sued for libel, charging that the remarks had reduced his income from $1,100,000 in 1937 to $810,000 in 1938. But the jury was unsympathetic. It agreed with Dr. Fishbein that charlatan and quack were not libelous terms when applied to "Goat-Gland" Brinkley.

Jarred by these various exposures, Brinkley's patients began reassessing the benefits of their goat glands, mercurochrome, and indigo. They started suing and winning judgments against him.

Minnie was frightened but her audacious husband assured her that the tempest was temporary. He sold an airplane to some Britons to pay off a few verdicts, then sold a yacht to the president of Venezuela for $125,000. Then the cars were disposed of one by one, next the Little Rock hospital, and finally his last airplane, for which the U. S. Navy gave him $119,000.

Now fifty-four, Brinkley reached in desperation for any political handhold that was convenient. He gave $5,000 to William Dudley Pelley, leader of the anti-Semitic Silver Shirts, and urged him to ferret out Communists and publicity with it.

He also had his astrological chart prepared regularly and one month in 1940 it told him gigantic things were ahead. He interpreted this to mean he should run for President of the United States and Minnie announced he had received 500,000 letters urging him to do so. But two fellows named Roosevelt and Willkie ran instead.

In February, 1941, weighed down by judgments and the countless dollars that had been paid under the table during his circuitous career, Brinkley was bankrupt. The Federal Court at San Antonio estimated his assets to be $221,065 and his liabilities at $1,625,565. Despite this blow, his name appeared the following June as a candidate for Texas's Democratic nomination for U. S. senator, opposing such people as Governor W. Lee, "Pappy" O'Daniel, and Lyndon Johnson. William Allen White lathered up again and wrote: "He is irresistible to the moron mind, and Texas has plenty of such."

But few people cared. Brinkley was no longer an issue. In August, he suffered a coronary occlusion and entered a hospital in Kansas City, where his left leg was amputated. In May, 1942, at fifty-six, Goat-Gland Brinkley dropped dead.

He could claim as distinction that he rifled the pockets of 20,000 wistful men for a net of roughly $10,000,000, helped Alf Landon to a chance at the U. S. presidency, and almost became the first American spellbinder to reach a political position of high standing. The goat-man was no piker.

Minnie Brinkley was at her husband's side to the end. Her reverence had not faltered during his downhill slide and she had never been heard to complain that he needed any goat gland rejuvenation himself. Minnie was a satisfied woman, and she paid scant attention to catcalls that greeted her on the streets of Kansas City.

Well, actually they were goat calls. The jokers shouted, "Ba-a-a!"

CHAPTER IV

Andrew Carnegie's Wild Oats

O N CHRISTMAS DAY, 1904, thousands of
American parents sent their children off
to fight over the wishbones so they could relish the story
of Cassie Chadwick without inhibition.

Cassie had been the new century's Elsa Maxwell of
party givers, the Babs Hutton of spenders. By Thanksgiving Day of 1904, she had also become the central figure
in a colossal financial mystery. By Christmas almost everyone realized that the dazzling Society Queen of Cleveland
—the confidante of bankers—was the most spectacular
female swindler the United States had ever seen.

If Cassie was not bold, she was nothing. She represented
herself as the wild-oat child of bachelor Andrew Carnegie
and implied that the steel baron was making huge, discreet
payments for his youthful waywardness. On the strength
of this elaborate fraud, she robbed rich men of about
$2,000,000. The rich men helped her by allowing their
greed to obscure their good sense, but that was not unex-
pected; it was one of the frailties of human nature she had
counted on.

Cassie was not always Cassie. She was born in 1857, the third daughter of Daniel and Mary Ann Bigley near London, Ontario, not far from Detroit. Daniel was a farmer who held a part-time job as a railroad section hand to compensate for the meager return of the soil. The new daughter, Elizabeth, grew into a child who perplexed her parents. Her imagination was so boundless, they frequently worried over her sanity. She kept to herself, read endlessly about the lives of the fashionable women of the world, and decided that their status was her goal.

Aware that her family lived on the edge of poverty, she realized she would have to acquire money of her own. And so it followed that at the age of fifteen, she spent a half hour with a young farmer who had long been trying to attract her attention. During their first brook-side date, she held him off long enough to negotiate her first big deal. The farmer offered to mortgage his land so he could buy her a diamond—something she had always wanted. In return, she agreed to return to the brook and spend a night with him. Later, the enthusiastic young farmer asked her to marry him, but Elizabeth said no—that was not part of the deal.

The diamond kept the girl's dreams under control for three years, when, one Saturday morning, she visited nearby London for a weekend of shopping. After making her selections at several shops, she raised cash by presenting the proprietors with checks written for larger amounts than her purchases. When they asked for identification, she presented a small business card that, for its simplicity, commands awe. It read:

Miss Bigley

Heiress to $15,000

Several managers were taken aback, but all of them eventually ascribed the gauche nature of this message to the youth of its charming bearer. She had blonde curls, her manner was delicate, and her choices of merchandise were exceptionally tasteful. All hands came through with both merchandise and cash. So Elizabeth spent the balance of the weekend promenading through the town and luxuriating in a costly hotel suite.

On Monday afternoon, as she was preparing to leave for the drabness of home, the police arrived. The banks had notified the shop managers that they held no account for a Miss Bigley. Elizabeth, appearing utterly mystified, accompanied the officers to the constabulary, where she was confronted by the agitated shopkeepers. When they discovered she had only enough money left to return home, they decided it would not be worth their trouble to press charges. Elizabeth left peaceably, taking with her the clothes the store managers did not bother to repossess.

As her sisters married and left home, she continued to be the odd child, hidden away in her room, studying books and magazines. But at twenty-two, she embarked on another fling. This time she chose Toronto, where she initiated operations by making out a check to herself and signing it with a name recalled from a romantic story. She opened a bank account with the check and began writing checks on it herself.

But banks work quickly in Toronto, and one day later Miss Bigley was lodged in jail. Thoroughly respectful now of the need for thought in dealing with financial institutions, she elected to admit or deny nothing. A week later, when she came to trial, she sat mutely, wearing a childish bonnet and a blank, frightened expression. The judge, who was fond of youngsters, directed the jury to acquit her on grounds of insanity. Then he ruled she was no longer insane and sent her home.

The Bigleys could stand no more. They packed Elizabeth off to Cleveland to board with a daughter who was living the morally invigorating life of a new bride. That is how the United States got Cassie Chadwick for its own. For a quarter-century after her arrival, Cassie made Cleveland her base of operations in a never-ending campaign against men who had money.

Although the married Bigley sister soon had Elizabeth meeting all the handsome young eligibles, no romance developed. It was not the men's fault; several of them jockeyed about for her favor. But, as she explained to her sister, she was holding out for the right man.

While waiting, she needed spending money, so she borrowed some, putting up her sister's new furniture as security. On the day sister discovered this alarming situation, Elizabeth arrived home with an overshadowing announcement. An up-and-coming young doctor had proposed and she was about to become Mrs. Wallace Springsteen. In the confusion of happiness, mortgaged-furniture problems were dismissed.

On the seventh day of his marriage, Dr. Springsteen found a sheriff waiting for him at his front door. It developed that, in the months before she met the doctor, Elizabeth had run up a fantastic schedule of bills around Cleveland; the creditors had learned of the marriage and were attaching everything he owned. Springsteen, disenchanted with his blonde, petite wife, went home to his mother, who suggested he put private detectives on the bride's trail. He did and three months later he had no trouble obtaining a divorce on grounds of adultery.

Elizabeth learned from this experience that the fox does not virtually summon the hounds, as she had done. Mulling this thought, she decided to try her luck in Toledo, which was then a carnival ground for clairvoyants, faith healers, and other scamps. She set up shop as Madame Lydia Devere, a fortune teller with supernatural powers. The occupation proved lucrative and she stayed at it for seven years, when she decided to throw her whole body into the business of making money.

It was then that Elizabeth rediscovered sex, to which she added an enticing fillip. She assumed various identities, each of them noble and exciting. As a result, one man thought he was seducing the daughter of a British general, another the widow of an earl. And a wealthy young Ohioan was delighted to be subtly blackmailed by the niece of General U. S. Grant who, all the newspapers reported, was having financial troubles at the time. The opportunity to bail out a former president through his pretty niece does not come to many Americans.

Whether it was bigger money or more excitement that spurred her, Elizabeth then devised a scheme that required the services of an accomplice. She located an express clerk, a young, wide-eyed fellow who liked to read poetry with her in her apartment. Before long—in fact, without knowing exactly how it came about—he had seduced her. Elizabeth, now thirty, mothered him through a period of remorse over his betrayal of his wife. Then she went to work.

She produced a note for $2,000 signed by someone the young man had not heard of but who, she assured him, was a prominent Cleveland businessman. Obligingly, the clerk walked the note to the nearest bank and cashed it. Two weeks later he cashed one for $4,000 and, before long, the total came to $40,000 at nine banks. Then he was arrested.

Knowledge comes hard and to Elizabeth, or Madame Devere, it still did not come quickly. Repeating her mistake with Dr. Springsteen in Cleveland, she overstayed her grace in Toledo. When the express clerk had sobbed out his story to the police, she was easily available. In court, she attempted the confused-silence gambit once more, but it was no longer adequate. The clerk's lawyer laid out the story of his client's poetic trysts with Madame Devere, described the seduction in such a way that she was clearly the aggressor, and added that his marriage was ruined and he was a broken man. The jury sent the clerk home and the judge sent forger Lydia Devere to the Ohio Penitentiary for nine and a half years.

With little to do in her cell in Columbus, Elizabeth devoted herself to a stern, disciplined review of her errors. It was not the kind of review the prison chaplain would have suggested, but that is neither here nor there. Elizabeth concluded that what she needed to bring the world to its knees was a magnificent plan, one startling enough to balk disbelief.

Having settled on her design, she opened a campaign of inspired letter writing to the State Parole Board. She had learned her lesson, she said, and wanted freedom only to prove that she could earn the right to hold her head high once more. The letters were so moving that they were forwarded to the State Capitol where, just before Christmas, 1893, Governor William McKinley signed her parole papers. Elizabeth Bigley Springsteen Devere scampered back to Cleveland, where she snipped ties with her past by becoming Mrs. Cassie L. Hoover, a widow.

Living comfortably enough on the proceeds of her financial raids, the Widow Hoover bided her time until 1896, when she was thirty-nine and looked like thirty-three, which she claimed to be. It was then that she met a Cleveland surgeon, Dr. Leroy Chadwick, whose successful practice was more serene than his private life. His wife had died, his chronically ill mother lived in his fashionable home on Euclid Avenue, and an invalid sister now lived with him, too. Cassie was nice to them and to the doctor's young daughter as well. He needed her charm and pleasantness around the house, and so, he soon proposed marriage. She blushed and accepted.

Mrs. Cassie Chadwick moved into Leroy's lavish West Side home and quickly established herself as the matron of the mansion. Personal servants flocked around her and, in addition to a handsome carriage, she enjoyed the use of her own car—this, in the pioneering days of the automobile industry.

Night after night she staged parties for the most prominent people in town. Between goblets of champagne, she offered her share of bright small talk, but she also listened attentively to the local gossip. She was ebullient, personable, and she radiated good cheer. Soon Cassie was a popular member of the clubby set.

But for the farm girl from Ontario, this was small game. As the revelry grew, she became more and more the quiet, thoughtful hostess. Cassie was thinking. She was learning about life among the wealthy and wondering how best to put its weaknesses to her advantage. She was seeking a grand swindle and late in 1901, the idea suddenly jelled.

Preparing carefully for the opening move of her plot, she neglected no detail. She visited the Euclid Avenue Baptist Church with unflagging regularity and thus won the affection of its pastor, the Reverend Charles Eaton. The good man probably would have burned his church down the day he met her, if he could have known where this friendship would lead to.

By Easter, 1902, Cassie was ready for action. Taking a well-selected and very garrulous Cleveland attorney with her, she entrained for New York. There she hired a hansom and escorted him up Fifth Avenue. The lawyer was curious about his mission, but Cassie would say nothing. At Fifty-ninth Street, before a magnificent mansion, the carriage halted and she got out.

"I'll be but a few minutes," she said. She walked through the iron gates and up to the massive oak door of what everybody who was anybody knew to be the home of Andrew Carnegie. The lawyer's mystification became amazement as the door opened and Cassie was shown in.

In the housekeeper's drawing room, Cassie was spinning the time away discussing a maid's references. The girl had come to her, she said, claiming she had been in Carnegie's employ; and Cassie, while in New York, was checking up. She seemed chagrined to learn that the girl's name was unknown in the household, and left with profuse thanks for the housekeeper's help. On the way out, she removed a package from a large handbag and carried it under her arm.

When she entered the carriage again, the lawyer fumed. "My dear Mrs. Chadwick," he said, "I realize I am being well paid, but I have done nothing to earn it and an ethical lawyer should understand the reason for his fee. I must insist you disclose the nature of your business with Mr. Carnegie."

Cassie blushed. She had chosen both her men well. The lawyer could be counted on to spread the story once he knew it and Carnegie's name would insure wide interest and excitement. Staring out the carriage window, she spoke in awkward embarrassment. "This can never pass beyond you," she said. "You must promise that first."

The lawyer promised.

"Have you ever noticed the painting of an elderly man at the top of the main staircase of my home?" she asked.

Yes, he had. It was a striking portrait of a distinguished, white-bearded man with a strong face.

"He was my uncle. On his deathbed he told me a secret he felt he could keep from me no longer." She blushed again and then blurted the key piece of the entire affair.

"I am Mr. Carnegie's daughter."

"My God!" the lawyer breathed. Then he exclaimed, "But Mr. Carnegie isn't married!" He paused. "Oh dear. Oh, Mrs. Chadwick!"

Cassie was crimson. Tears formed. "My father was so attached to his mother that he would never marry. She forbade it. So he developed a relationship with my mother that had to be hidden from his own mother. When I was born, they kept it a secret. I don't even know who my mother is." She seemed about to faint.

"I must speak to you frankly," the lawyer said. "Does Mr. Carnegie acknowledge you as his daughter?"

Cassie nodded. She handed him the package she carried.

With it were two notes, one of which read: "One year after date, I promise to pay to Cassie L. Chadwick $25,000, with interest at five percent."

The note was dated January 7, 1904, which was almost two years away, and was signed "Andrew Carnegie" in a huge scrawl. The second note was for $500,000. Both signatures appeared to be the ironmaster's, the lawyer concluded. He berated himself for having momentarily suspected otherwise.

"What's in the package?" he asked.

Cassie had rehearsed well. "Securities in the value of $5,000,000."

When she sent the lawyer back to Cleveland so she could enjoy a few days' shopping in Manhattan, he was her property.

By the time she returned to the Euclid Avenue house the story had been spread from his law offices to the most exclusive parlors in town. She was greeted with exceptional sympathy and understanding, and Cassie chuckled as she intercepted glances of intimate knowledge.

A few days later she called on Iri Reynolds, treasurer of the Wade Park Bank, one of Cleveland's most respected private financial institutions. In the privacy of his office, Cassie handed him the package. When he regarded her with awkward compassion, it was obvious that he was also in the know. Reynolds pressed for no details beyond Cassie's assertion that $5,000,000 in stocks and bonds lay beneath the string and wrapping paper. He handed her a note reading: "I hereby certify that I have in my possession $5,000,000 in securities belonging to Mrs. Cassie L. Chadwick, and that neither myself nor the Wade Park

Bank nor any other person has any claim upon the same. Iri Reynolds."

Moving into second gear, Cassie went to her pastor, Charles Eaton, and confessed her secret. Since the pastor was already aware of it, he was proud of Cassie for trusting him. And he also felt impelled to help her raise some immediate cash on the strength of her securities. So he passed her name on to his brother, Boston lawyer John Eaton.

Soon Cassie received a note from a Boston investment banker, Herbert D. Newton, who said he might be in a position to lend a large sum of money. Cassie hurried to Boston and laid Iri Reynolds' trust receipt on Newton's desk. When she also exhibited $750,000 in pre-dated notes signed with Andrew Carnegie's name, Newton stuttered in excitement. He handed her a check for $79,000 and his own note, good at any bank, for $50,000 more. In return for this one year, $129,000 loan, he presented a promissory note for $190,000. Cassie scanned it briefly, then signed. A profit of $61,000 meant she was being charged almost fifty percent interest. The greed amused her, the details were a bore. Cassie went home and turned banker Newton's personal note into cash.

The following Sunday, when she and Dr. Chadwick entered the Euclid Avenue Church, the Reverend Eaton beamed and Cassie deposited fifty dollars in the collection plate. The pastor walked them home after the service and heard Dr. Chadwick explain how well off they had become since he turned over all his financial affairs to his wife. Her investments were paying magnificent returns, he said. The pastor smiled; he was no man to give a supplicant's confidence away.

Now Elizabeth Bigley and her youthful squalor were dead. Cassie Chadwick was more than the wife of a well-to-do doctor. She was beginning to get rich, and everyone knew it, as her parties became more bacchanalian by the week. No one sat down to dinner without finding a tasteful souvenir under the napkin and no one left, drunk or sober, without receiving a costly gift. Cassie thrived on the admiration she earned, the attention that a mere farm girl could never have hoped to attract. She was *somebody* now.

Before 1902 was out, however, she discovered that living on such a scale demanded even more wealth than she had acquired. So she sought out more greedy men. She was like a later bandit, Willie Sutton, who, when asked why he always robbed banks, replied, "That's where the money is." When Cassie wanted to steal money, she went to banks.

This time, it was the Citizens National Bank of Oberlin, Ohio, where she found two upstanding community leaders in President Charles T. Beckwith and Cashier A. B. Spear.

Establishing her financial footing in the gentle manner, she exhibited the Iri Reynolds trust certificate and asked for a mere $10,000. Beckwith and Spear, finding her guileless, decided to make the loan out of their own pockets, at a sharp interest rate. Cassie didn't mind. A month later she was back for $10,000 more, and then for another $20,000. When she reached $102,000, the load became too much for personal resources and, grudgingly, the pair opened the bank's vault to Cassie. She invaded it for $700,000, surrendering a $500,000 Carnegie note as collateral. Her take was now over $900,000.

None of this financial maneuvering interrupted Cassie's

high living; it only increased the pace. She walked into a piano store one day and picked out an instrument she liked. "How many of these do you have?" she inquired.

The manager counted up. "Twenty-seven," he said.

"I'll take them all," she replied. She wrote out the names of twenty-seven friends to whom the pianos should be sent.

Cassie also toured London, Paris, Rome, and the other principal cities of Europe and, being lonely, took four young ladies with her. Transportation tickets alone came to $10,000 and on her return she paid $10,000 duty on her purchases. But at home, the Society Queen of Cleveland found she needed a new cook. Cassie had given the woman so many costly clothes that she had quit on grounds the work was undignified and tended to ruin her wardrobe.

When the first of her loans fell due, unflustered Cassie paid only the exorbitant interest and extended the principal for an additional year. When several loans came due during 1903, she looked up a Pittsburgh steel magnate and got $800,000 from him on the strength of the $250,000 Carnegie note and her highly respected word. The Savings & Deposit Bank of Elyria, Ohio, gave up $10,000 more; Oberlin College $75,000; and the First National Bank of Conneaut, Ohio, another $25,000. She was nearing the $2,000,000 mark and celebrated it at Christmas, 1903, by sending gifts to every child in the orphanages and foundling homes of Ohio.

The gift she gave Dr. Chadwick was a peek at his bank balance; he was flabbergasted and began to consider retiring. His were still the only prominent ears in Cleveland that had not received word of Cassie's supposed origins. Needless to say, neither had Andrew Carnegie's.

Cassie Chadwick's downfall was no less remarkable than her rise. Her scheme might have worked endlessly except for one of the inevitable flaws that accompany such manipulations—the impossible appetite of the manipulator. Cassie couldn't cut down and couldn't borrow enough to keep up. When the limit was reached, a shot fired from Boston was heard all the way to Ohio.

The debacle began at Eastertime, 1904, when another $61,000 interest payment fell due on her original $129,000 loan from Boston banker Newton. She could pay neither principal nor interest and Newton grew nervous. Cassie put him off with airy letters but, by midsummer, he was threatening legal action. At the same time President Beckwith and Cashier Spear of the Citizens National Bank of Oberlin began wondering about the wisdom of carrying $700,000 in Chadwick notes. They, too, asked her to settle up, but all they got was her smiling assurance that Andrew Carnegie was as good as his word.

Cassie went to New York, took a suite at the old Holland House, and brazenly embarked on a wild shopping spree.

The shot from Boston came just before Thanksgiving, when banker Newton sued for the full amount of his loan. He asked a Cleveland court to order Iri Reynolds of the Wade Park Bank to open Cassie's bundle of securities and turn $129,000 worth over to him. Three days later, when gossip had distorted the meaning of Newton's suit, Wade Park depositors opened a run on one of the bank's branch offices. They started lining up before Thursday's closing hour and Reynolds telephoned New York banks for cash. An automobile containing $75,000 left immediately and arrived in time to meet the run Friday morning.

At noon that day, Beckwith of the Oberlin bank, frightened and ill, confronted Cassie in New York and asked her to pay up. When she said she couldn't, he fainted at her feet. On Monday morning a sign on the door of the Citizens National Bank of Oberlin announced that the institution had failed. It had loaned Cassie forty times what banking laws allowed. Beckwith suffered a heart attack.

On Tuesday Carnegie's name was finally made public by banker Newton, and the aged millionaire, realizing the magnitude of the affair his name was involved in, snorted in disgust, "I have never heard of Mrs. Chadwick!" He refused to say another word.

The panic was on. Cassie disappeared from the Holland House amid rumors of suicide. Dr. Chadwick left for Europe with his daughter. Oberlin College pleaded for funds for seventy-five students who had deposited $25,000 in the Oberlin Bank. Iri Reynolds heightened the mystery by refusing to confirm or deny that he held Cassie's securities. Then a judge set the stage for a dramatic revelation by ordering Reynolds to bring Cassie's package to court. He did and when it was opened and found to contain nothing but worthless papers, he sat in the witness chair and cried openly.

When the judge asked how much money he had loaned Cassie himself, Reynolds' voice trembled. "Please excuse me from answering that question," he said. He was excused.

Cassie's fat was burning fiercely now, and the following week she was arrested in the Hotel Breslin in New York. Her arrest was as fantastic as her career. In her room, when police entered, was an attorney for John D. Rockefeller and the Standard Oil Company. He was only there to berate Cassie for having used his name to float one of her loans. But wagging tongues maintained that any associate of Rockefeller's was undoubtedly a secret emissary of Carnegie's.

Cassie took her downfall calmly, her big dark eyes staring directly ahead and her whitening hair bobbing gracefully as she walked beside a policeman. The officer found his duty unpleasant. "The kindest, gentlest face one would ever want to see," he told reporters. "Just such a face as you or I would like to see in our families."

Cassie's return to Cleveland was not triumphant. A crowd of 10,000, many of them bank depositors, greeted her at the railroad station with hoots, catcalls, and threats. Police fought the demonstrators back, Cassie collapsed, and she arrived at the County Jail on a stretcher.

Her wealthy friends told each other they always knew she was a phony. On Christmas Day, utterly abandoned, she ate a solitary dinner in her cell. On New Year's Day Dr. Chadwick returned from Europe, spent an hour with her, and departed with a chilly good-by.

The trial took place in March, after several bankers had been arrested for violating financial regulations and banker Beckwith had recovered from his heart attack only to kill himself. Former prisoners at the Ohio Penitentiary played their part by identifying Cassie as their forger friend, Lydia Devere, and Andrew Carnegie assured everyone that, while he had indeed been devoted to his mother, he had never fathered any clandestine children.

The jurors deliberated for two hours, then returned to demand dinner before they would deliver their verdict. Sated, they pronounced Cassie guilty. In March, 1905, while Andrew Carnegie was giving a huge chunk of his fortune to charity, Cassie was given ten years.

Six months later Dr. Chadwick, his practice ruined, obtained an annulment and moved to Florida to reestablish himself.

Cassie's end was as undistinguished as her beginning. She was a surly prisoner; once, when magician Harry Houdini played a benefit at the Ohio Penitentiary, she refused to attend his performance, preferring to sulk in her cell. She served two and a half years of her sentence and died in the prison hospital at the age of fifty—although by her spectacular reckoning she was only forty-four.

It is worth a footnote to explain what made Cassie so touchy during her incarceration. She was distressed because people were saying she had stolen the basic idea of her swindle from a Frenchwoman, Therese Daurignac. Cassie didn't appreciate that defamation at all—and, as a matter of fact, it wasn't justified, as a recapitulation of the Frenchwoman's story will show.

In 1882, Therese Daurignac declared that she had inherited $20,000,000 from an eccentric American businessman she had befriended some years earlier. He had remembered her kindness abundantly in his will, she explained.

Bundles of securities materialized in due time and so did a handsome husband, Frederic Humbert. Madame Therese Humbert thereupon heightened the intrigue by announcing that a second, conflicting will had been discovered, which allotted a share of the American's estate to two of his nephews. Immediately, all the securities were sealed in a safe amid tremendous publicity and Madame Humbert was ready to cash in.

On the strength of the supposed contents of the sealed safe, she borrowed $12,000,000 over the following twenty years and lived like Marie Antoinette. In June, 1902, when the safe was opened, it yielded a few trinkets and $1,000 worth of genuine securities. The imaginative lady got five years.

In 1905, careless readers glossed over the fact that the imprisoned Cassie Chadwick had put her scheme into motion at least six months before Madame Humbert was exposed. After reading of the Frenchwoman's sealed safe, Cassie had probably figured out the rest of the swindle herself, which was more than could be said of fifty million Frenchmen.

CHAPTER V

The Man Who Stole Most of New York

WHEN BILL TWEED was eighteen years old, the newspapers revealed that the Collector of the Port of New York had stolen $1,222,000 and fled to Europe.

Bill Tweed was shocked.

When Tweed was twenty-one and casting his first vote, he saw policemen chuckle as some men were paid to vote the right way and others were thrown out of polling places because they were unwilling to accept a bribe. And the next morning he read that 55,000 votes had been counted —in a city with 45,000 registered voters.

Bill Tweed was intrigued.

Fifteen years later, when Tweed was climbing the political ladder, he observed the methods of Fernando Wood, the most corrupt mayor New York City had ever had.

Bill Tweed marveled.

When Tweed eventually became boss of Tammany Hall, New York's Democratic Party organization, he emulated and outdid all the thieves who had preceded him. He helped himself to so much of the city's money, that no accurate count has ever been possible. With Runyonesque characters named "Brains" Sweeny, "Slippery Dick" Connolly, and "The Elegant One" Hall, he made off with at least $30,000,000; some estimates run as high as $200,-000,000.

And when "Boss" Tweed was finished, mortally ill and lying in a prison bed, he explained how it all had happened.

"New York City politics was always dishonest," he said. "A politician in coming forward takes things as they are. This population is too hopelessly split up into races and factions to govern except by the bribery of patronage, or by corruption."

Tweed's deathbed rationale held at least a grain of truth. He was himself a natural outgrowth of New York politics. It may well be that the last hurrah sounded in Boston, but there is no question that it first rang loud and clear from New York's Tammany Hall.

William Marcy Tweed learned something useful from every experience. Although it was not apparent to him or anyone else at the time, he began his political career at the age of twenty-five, in 1848, when he helped organize the Americus Engine Company No. 6, a beer drinking, water spouting volunteer fire association in lower Manhattan. A six-foot tall, 270 pound man of good cheer, he soon became the spirited chief of Big Six Americus. It was he who proposed that the fire buffs' water wagon be adorned with the head of a Bengal tiger, its fangs painted into a ferocious snarl and all details faithfully borrowed from a barbershop lithograph. The tiger later became Tammany Hall's emblem, but in those days was simply a reminder that the

Big Six was no group to be in the way of when it charged over the cobblestones in pursuit of flames.

The prevailing custom among rival fire companies was to stage water throwing contests on Saturday afternoons, the workingman's half day off. Tavern keepers obligingly erected towering pine trees before what they liked to call their refectories, and opposing firemen tried to squirt their streams over them. One Saturday, after Tweed had watched every fire company in the city fail to clear a huge tree in front of a West Side saloon, he predicted that the Big Six would do the trick easily.

That night he located a beached sailor along the Hudson River docks and offered him ten dollars to climb the tree and saw six feet off the top.

"Careful now," he said. "Clean up the sawdust when you're finished."

He gave the seaman only half the ten dollars and the following Friday night, when the stunting operation was to be performed, he retired early in preparation for the great event.

On Saturday afternoon he and seventy-five red-shirted volunteers pulled their wagon up before the tavern and Tweed surreptitiously inspected the ground beneath the tree. He could see no trace of sawdust. As he gave the signal a huge crowd roared, the pumpers laid onto the handles, and water rose in a magnificent stream. But it fell short of the treetop again and again. The mob jeered and he finally realized he'd been taken; the tree hadn't been cut at all.

When the angry fire fighter demanded an explanation from his operative, he learned his lesson.

"You only gave me half the money," the distrustful

sailor said, "so I climbed up and then climbed down again. I did half the job."

Tweed concluded that to avoid mishap, skulduggery should be paid for in full—and in advance. From that day forward he was a foresighted thief.

Marrying his boss' daughter the following year and settling down to fire fighting and clerking in a tobacco warehouse, the strapping young man paid little attention to politics except to vote Democratic at election time, as his chairmaker father did.

But Tammany Hall was ever watchful for popular young Democrats and, in 1850, one of its assemblymen asked him to run against the Whig candidate for assistant alderman of the Seventh Ward. Despite his political ignorance, Tweed knew the Democrats were badly divided at the time. But he grinned and said he'd do the favor. He lost by forty-seven votes, and the surprisingly slim margin made him realize that he would have won but for an insurgent Democrat running against him, who had split the anti-Whig vote.

Having given their horse a trial run in a cheap race, the pleased ward heelers prevailed on Tweed to become a candidate for alderman the following spring. This provided the youngster with an opportunity to demonstrate that he had learned a political trick. He called on a friend, a Whig, and induced him to enter the race as an independent candidate. On Election Day, the obliging friend split the Whig vote just enough to let Tweed squeak into the Common Council by forty-eight votes.

That was 1851, the opening year of a double decade in which the honest chairmaker's son proved that if a man

really sets his heart on plundering the City of New York,
life can be bountiful.

The Common Council in which Tweed sat consisted of
forty aldermen and assistant aldermen who wielded enormous power. They appointed policemen, granted or withheld business licenses and franchises, and could win the
last word over the mayor by overriding his veto.

The Council was the fount of municipal corruption
when Tweed joined it. Within weeks his bluff personality
made him its acknowledged leader, and within months his
growing imagination earned the body the sobriquet of
"The Forty Thieves." He and Whig Mayor Ambrose
Kingsland showed the way to corruption by ignoring their
party differences long enough to buy a piece of real estate
that the city needed for a paupers' burial ground. They
paid $30,000 for the land and sold it to their constituents
for $103,000. For the first time in his life, Tweed had an
impressive amount of money in the bank.

The balance of the year consisted of pettier but con-
sistent pillage. In July, when the body of elder statesman
Henry Clay lay in state at City Hall, the Council voted
to ship the remains to Albany aboard a Hudson River
steamer which the city would charter. Cigars and wine
came to $1,400 and black bunting cost the city $2,500,
but few of these items ever reached the steamer. Later
that year a man applied for a franchise to conduct a ferry
service between Manhattan and Brooklyn, then an independent municipality. The franchise was granted when
the thoughtful man paid a bribe of $20,000 and lined up
Brooklyn's Democrats in support of Bill Tweed's next
aspiration—a seat in the U. S. House of Representatives.

The election was a breeze but Washington was a bore. Tweed was used to action and deals, and these are not what come the way of a freshman congressman. He was ignored. What was worse, he feared New York City might begin ignoring him. So he divided his time between Washington and the outside rail of his first love, the Common Council. That station held the special pleaders, the lobbyists, and the favor purchasers—the men who made money exciting.

Tweed also studied the actions of Fernando Wood, then the Democratic mayor of New York. Wood had amassed a fortune from grog shops, gambling interests, and shipping vessels. He was an artful demagogue who liked to reiterate that too many New Yorkers were "in want of the necessaries of life." He damned the city's dependence on free-roaming hogs to clean up the garbage in the streets, and he demanded that the checkrein legislature in Albany grant the city more freedom to chart its own destiny. The legislators made Wood popular by refusing, and helped him further by trying to saddle the city with Prohibition.

Tweed watched the Mayor's many brazen thefts, but he also watched Wood's status rise and fall in Tammany Hall. The Mayor's weakness lay in his lust for personal power, as opposed to power based in Tammany and administered in an organized way. Wood's greed caused large numbers of Tammany leaders to plot his downfall. Tweed, with the eye of a hawk, saw in the anti-Wood campaign a chance to consolidate his own rising power. He took his first step by forming an alliance with a pair of Tammany's nimblest hacks, Richard B. Connolly and Peter B. Sweeny.

Connolly, known even to his friends as "Slippery Dick,"

was an immigrant who had been an obscure bank clerk dabbling in ward politics. He had been drafted by Tammany to keep the Irish vote in line and had ascended to behind-the-scenes power. He was not a clever man, but he knew how to shake a hand, and how to vote a man four times in one day.

"Brains" Sweeny, a scholarly lawyer, was a big, heavy, bushy-browed man with no affection for people, of whom there were 750,000 in New York. Connolly would admonish him, "Sweeny, you've got a boiled shirt for a heart." He spent many evenings taking instruction from Connolly in the art of handshaking and smiling.

So Slippery Dick, Brains, and Bill Tweed joined hands and waited for Mayor Wood to slip. Wood's second term, beginning in 1857, was so wantonly corrupt that the legislators in Albany decided to strip his administration of some of its powers. They created a twelve member Board of Supervisors and tried to insure it against dishonesty by making it bipartisan. Six members would be Democrats and six would be Republicans (who had absorbed the Whigs). In theory, Democrats would vote for their own, Republicans for theirs, and one would watch the other. In practice, one *washed* the other, for Tammany's Tweed immediately bought the vote of one of the Republican Supervisors for $2,500. Thus, the balance of power was destroyed almost as soon as it was created.

In the 1858 election out of which the first Board of Supervisors took office, Tammany also managed to beat Fernando Wood by pitting a machine candidate against him. Wood was so thoroughly despised that even Republicans and independents voted the Tammany choice in order to unseat him.

Tweed was impressed that against such opposition Wood lost by only 2,500 out of 84,000 votes. He silently thanked the defeated man for teaching him one more trick—a new process for manufacturing American citizens. For Wood had sent 4,000 immigrants to a cooperative judge, who signed the necessary papers by the ream and swore them in by the hundreds. The aliens, many of whom were unhappy over discovering that New York was not paved with gold after all, found renewed happiness in their naturalization and voted for their benefactor. Wood's only error was in underestimating by 2,501 the number of new citizens he would need. Tweed decided he would always count more carefully.

Meanwhile, he had things to be grateful for. The election that ousted Wood made Sweeny district attorney and Connolly county clerk.

But after being out of office for only one term, Fernando Wood staged a comeback in 1860, by manipulating the minorities and damning Abraham Lincoln, who only became popular in New York once he was dead. This was of small concern to Bill Tweed, who was then being called "Big Bill" Tweed. He had been cementing his power in Tammany Hall and preparing to take a seat himself on the Board of Supervisors. He had also added another cabinet member to his ring—A. Oakey Hall, known as "The Elegant One."

Hall was a sophisticate, an anti-Lincoln Republican turned Democrat. He was a lawyer, a playwright, a brilliant, witty cynic and the smartest dresser in town. He knew everybody who was anybody and wanted only one material thing from life: money. In Tweed he saw the source of it, and in The Elegant One, Tweed saw a compliant, irreproachable front man.

As Wood returned to the mayor's office and Tweed became a supervisor, Oakey Hall joined Sweeny and Connolly behind the Ring's scenes. A decade of debauchery set in, with Tweed commanding the raiders. Examples: he bought three hundred meeting benches for $1,500 and sold them to the city for $169,000. He paid $3,080 for a quarry and supplied marble for a courthouse for $420,000. He sold appointments, bartered franchises, and bribed the press. The Tweed Ring made millions and through its control of ballot counters and election inspectors, it stood in little danger of retribution.

In 1866 Tweed elected to expand. The legislature controlled much of the city's finances and also dictated its right to levy taxes. So, he distributed boodle in the wards, ran for the State Senate, and was elected handily. By the time he took office, he was also president of the Supervisors, the city's education commissioner and assistant street commissioner, and the most powerful political figure in the state next to the chairman of the Democratic State Committee, Samuel J. Tilden. The governor didn't count.

Ignoring Tilden whenever possible, which was often, Tweed established his Albany headquarters in a hotel suite. Six rooms held huge liquor sideboards; a seventh housed his bed, flowers, canaries, and cuspidors. His regular visitors were Connolly, Sweeny, and Hall, whose task it was to inspect all pending legislation for possibilities of graft. No such laws were enacted until Slippery Dick, Brains, and The Elegant One had collected the Ring's proper price. Enough Republicans played ball to make it all possible.

Tweed also introduced a game that the legislators enjoyed. It was known as "ringing the bell," but it was not for children. In "ringing the bell," a legislator introduced a bill that would be damaging to an industry. The industry heard the bell ring and arrived in Albany with cash while the appropriate committee was considering the bill. Soon the bell stopped ringing.

From his seat in this pleasant game room, Tweed raised his sights. With Albany in his pocket, he could return to New York City and take over. Returning would be easy; taking over called for the sort of maneuver at which he was becoming adept.

The year was 1868 and the governorship was at stake. Tammany had won the Democratic gubernatorial nomination for its incumbent New York mayor, John T. Hoffman, but a quick survey of the state presented a dilemma that afflicts New York City Democrats even today. Hoffman could carry the city, but not by a big enough margin to offset the expected Republican vote in the upstate counties. So Tweed concentrated on the problem of overcoming this obstacle and making Hoffman governor.

"Figure me the upstate bulge," he told Sweeny.

Sweeney figured and said a Republican margin of 40,000 votes would have to be overcome.

"You can't pack ballot boxes that full," observed Connolly.

"I know," The Boss said, "but immigration has been high."

Everyone nodded. They reminisced over Fernando

Wood's contributions to the American melting pot ten years earlier and remembered that he had underestimated the number of new citizens he needed.

Over the previous decade, an average of 6,000 aliens had been naturalized each year, but within twenty days after Mayor Hoffman was nominated for governor, 60,000 of Emma Lazarus' huddled masses gratefully became American citizens. One judge alone created 37,000 voters; true, a court clerk had helped by mastering the judge's scrawl, but that was just a technicality and probably a humanitarian one at that. What judge could count his money after signing almost 2,000 naturalization forms a day for twenty days? And how could every necessary article be in its right place at the right time? It couldn't, and one day, when a judge couldn't find a Bible, he swore citizens in with a copy of *A New Method of Learning to Read, Write and Speak French*.

The consequence of these and other Tammany procedures was that on New Year's Day, 1869, Boss Tweed owned much more than his seats in the State Senate and the New York County Board of Supervisors. He owned Governor Hoffman. And he owned the new mayor of New York, The Elegant One Hall. Connolly had become controller and Sweeney the court chamberlain. A man named George Barnard had ascended to the State Supreme Court bench and a hack named James O'Brien was now New York County sheriff.

Tweed owned them all, and to close the Ring, he set out to gain absolute control of Tammany Hall too. He accomplished this feat by packing its meetings with thugs and demanding unanimity. Once, for example, he insisted that a vote had been unanimously affirmative but couldn't be heard over the roar of "noes." So he adjourned the meeting and left; when the negative voters tried to carry on, he had the gas turned off. The vote was recorded as unanimous.

Early in 1869, Boss Tweed owned Tammany Hall.

Municipal thievery could now be carried forward in a highly relaxed manner, since all bookkeeping was being handled in the family. So Tweed informed each of the city's and county's suppliers that henceforth all bills were to be raised to specified amounts. The suppliers would be allowed to keep a percentage of the inflation; the balance, the lion's share, would go to the Ring.

The arrangement was effective, as two examples demonstrate: one firm collected $1,063,498 for furniture, only a few pieces of which were delivered. And a contractor collected $646,516 for repairs to the plaster in one building.

The Ring was stealing an average of one million dollars a month.

Tweed earned even more as a personal entrepreneur. He became intimate with financier Jay Gould and was a director of Gould's and James Fisk's Tenth National Bank and of their Erie Railroad. He did legislative chores for them in Albany and helped defraud stockholders in the notorious Erie treasury looting. He was also president of a bank and a director of several utilities.

To all these activities of the Democratic boss, the Republicans seemed oblivious; fifty-nine of their leaders were on the Tweed payroll.

There remained only one nail to drive home and Tweed drove it during the spring of 1870. He won for the city a Home Rule Charter, which gave it more financial independence than it had ever known. He won it by distributing $600,000 among Albany legislators of both parties, who thereupon created a Board of Audit. Its members consisted of Tweed, Hall, Connolly, and Sweeny. Every nickel that entered or left the city's treasury had to pass through the four-man Ring.

The Ring decided it was entitled to one of every three dollars the city spent. The Boss, The Elegant One, Slippery Dick, and Brains each took twenty percent, and used the remainder for bribes. One month after the arrangement began, the Ring increased its take to fifty percent. Then, when Connolly demanded a larger share because, after all, he was the city controller and a key figure, the graft percentage became two-thirds. Finally it leveled off at eighty-five percent; out of every dollar the city paid out, eighty-five cents was kicked back to the Ring.

That was the end of restraint. One meeting of the Board of Audit approved payment of $6,312,500, of which $5,300,000 went to the gang. A $3,000,000 courthouse cost the taxpayers $12,000,000. The Manufacturing Stationers' Company collected $3,000,000; one of its bills, for $10,000, covered twelve reams of paper, two dozen penholders, four bottles of ink, a dozen sponges, and three dozen boxes of rubber bands. Tweed owned the company.

The man was no longer the chairmaker's son, the gallused fireman with a tree-shrinking prank in mind. Nor was he a struggling, sandwich-eating politician. He had learned to worship opulence, and now he never appeared in public without a shirt front of diamonds. Pleasant weekends were spent aboard his yacht, and he and his wife and son rode from the docks to their mansion at Fifth Avenue and Fifty-ninth Street in a custom-built carriage. He was paunchy and heading for fifty, but he walked with the step of a thirty-year-old. Boss Tweed was in the prime of his life.

From reading the press, one would think it was the life of a saint or, at the very least, of a municipal reformer. Tweed fed the newspapers official advertising at a dollar a line—$2,700,000 worth in two and a half years—and the lady of truth became a mistress. Albany was well in hand, too. The legislature had its laws printed in newspaper shops there, and the income of one Tweed-dominated paper, the *Argus*, is revealing. In 1868 it had received $5,000 worth of work; in 1870 it collected $176,000.

There were exceptions, yes. There was *Harper's Weekly*, in which cartoonist Thomas Nast repeatedly crucified Tweed with his pen. And there was the New York *Times* which, for a good while, exemplified honesty in chains. Its editor, George Jones, frothed to get at The Boss, but one of the *Times*' directors was, of all things, a Tweed partner in a printing firm that shook the city down for $7,000,000. He was James B. Taylor, and because of him Jones had to content himself with infrequent, tangential sideswipes.

In the fall of 1870, however, Taylor double-crossed Tweed by dying and Jones double-crossed Taylor's memory by initiating a campaign of truth, vividly stated. Republican Jones charged that "notoriously corrupt Republicans" had sold out to Tweed and that the city was "at the mercy of reckless plunderers."

If Tweed was disturbed by such broadsides, he didn't show it. In fact, his arrogance grew by the day until he made the blunder that seems to climax so many successful careers in crime. He cheated one of his own gang. He held out $350,000 which Sheriff James O'Brien said he was entitled to for being such a cooperative lawman.

"The man is dishonest," Tweed told Brains Sweeny. "He's charging for things he hasn't done. Walk over and tell him to go to hell." Sweeny did. So O'Brien set out to collect his money in another way. He planted a spy in the county auditor's office and told him to filch the most incriminating evidence he could find. The spy, Matthew J. O'Rourke, was a foresighted man. He made copies of the evidence for himself. He, too, aspired to the evidence-selling business.

In June, 1871, Sheriff O'Brien dropped into the offices of the *Sun* with documented information for sale. He failed to find a taker. He tried to sell the information elsewhere, but a half-dozen newspapers later, he was a discouraged and angry man. On the evening of July 4th, he went to the *Times*. There he found managing editor Louis John Jennings reading proofs and perspiring. The sheriff remarked on the humidity, then plunged into the business at hand.

"You and Nast have had a hard fight," he said.

"Still have," Jennings replied.

"Had," O'Brien insisted. He tossed his documents on Jennings' desk and left.

A few days later, while Jennings and George Jones were constructing a news bombshell, O'Brien's spy, Matthew J. O'Rourke, walked in with his copies of the evidence; O'Rourke also had some originals that he hadn't even given Sheriff O'Brien.

On July 8th the bombardment began. "Gigantic Frauds in the Rental of Armories," a *Times'* headline said. "Eighty

Per Cent of the Money Stolen." The story revealed that about $90,000,000 a year in municipal funds was passing through the hands of Tweed and his men, and that most of it was remaining with them. The city was renting tiny taverns and over-the-stable rooms as "armories," and "repairs" to these premises were running into the hundreds of thousands of dollars.

With a strong editorial flavor, the article pinpointed the Ring's responsibility:

Who are responsible for these frauds? First, Mayor Hall and Controller Connolly, who pass upon these claims and sign checks for their payment—knowing them to be fraudulent. Second, William M. Tweed and Peter B. Sweeny, who pocket their share of the proceeds—knowing them to have been fraudulently obtained.

Now Tweed realized that the *Times* held damaging information. His logical reaction was to order the purchase of Editor Jones. He also decided that Cartoonist Nast should study painting in Europe for five years and offered him $100,000 a year for living expenses. But Nast replied that he was more interested in the art of political cartooning at the moment. As for Jones, it seemed impossible to arrange a meeting with the man; he was simply too busy. So one day Slippery Dick Connolly contrived to have the editor drop into a lawyer's office. Connolly was waiting in an adjoining office and stepped out as Jones entered. The old *Harper's Weekly* described the scene this way:

"I don't want to see this man," said Mr. Jones, and he turned to go.

"For God's sake!" exclaimed Connolly. "Let me say one word to you."

At this appeal Mr. Jones stopped. Connolly then made him a proposition to forego the publication of the documents he had in his possession and offered him the enormous sum of five million dollars to do this. As Connolly waited for the answer Mr. Jones said:

"I don't think the devil will ever make a higher bid for me than that."

Connolly began to plead, and drew a graphic picture of what one could do with five million dollars. He ended by saying:

"Why, with that sum you could go to Europe and live like a prince."

"Yes," said Mr. Jones, "but I should know that I was a rascal."

The somewhat romantic dialogue of that conversation has been perpetuated in newspaper lore. Whether it was more earthily carried on or not, the fact is that Jones spurned the bribe offer and earned a place in fourth-estate history.

On July 22, the *Times* impaled Tweed on Page One under the headline: "THE SECRET ACCOUNTS." The article showed that $5,600,000 had been paid for repairs and furniture for a new courthouse, that a carpenter had drawn $360,000 for one month's work, and that a plasterer, Andrew J. Garvey, had collected almost $1,000,000 for two months' labor. The *Times* dubbed Garvey "The Prince of Plasterers" and showed that between fifty and eighty-five percent of millions of dollars in preposterous overcharges had gone to Tweed's Ring.

Day after day the stories went on, with the *World* accusing the *Times* of "a reckless attempt to shake and undermine the city credit." Boss Tweed, however, knew who was being undermined, but he put on a fierce show of bravado. When a reporter questioned him about the disclosures he did not bother to deny them. Instead, he retorted brazenly, "Well, what are you going to do about it?"

But it seems obvious in retrospect that this most practical of men knew the jig was up. He was immediately betrayed by a judge who issued an injunction that froze city payments. The Boss began transferring his assets to friends and family. Connolly felt the ship pitching in the political storm and made a deal with Tweed's opposition that let them put a spy into his own office. The unhampered spy brought out more evidence. Meanwhile, Tweed had himself reelected to the State Senate, but he was only going through the motions.

In November, Sweeny suddenly decided to winter in France, and Garvey, "the Prince of Plasterers," went with him. Mayor Hall began talking to Tweed's enemy, Samuel J. Tilden, the State Democratic boss. Tilden had his eye on the governorship, with the U. S. presidency further along the horizon, and Tweed's downfall seemed a convenient campaign issue.

A Grand Jury indicted The Boss and, in December, 1871, he was arrested. Bail was set at $1,000,000 ($2,000,-000 if in real estate) but Tweed didn't spend a night in jail; Jay Gould alone put up half the amount. Connolly, to his surprise, was indicted, too, but as soon as he had bailed himself out for $500,000, he fled to France.

With no one in the way, Tilden took control of Tammany Hall.

Indictments against Tweed came down for a year, during which time he talked of jury buying. No one knows whether he did pocket the jury that tried him in January, 1873, but it did not agree on a verdict. He greeted his dismissal with a sneer. "I'm tired of the whole farce," he said. "No jury will ever convict me."

But he was indicted again and tried the following November on two hundred and twenty counts of embezzlement and forgery. This time conviction was swift on two hundred and four of the counts. The Boss was dethroned!

One of his appointees took his hand before the sentencing and said, "I hope you will bear up, Bill."

Tweed murmured, "Ah, I have tried to bear up. I never thought it would come to this."

He sounded like a child up for cookie stealing.

Perhaps it was this attitude that had kept Tweed from following his partners and henchmen to Europe, or perhaps flight was simply not in his code. In any event, he stood calmly before the bench in the courthouse that graft built and received a fine of $12,750 and a term of twelve years in jail.

The man was not yet broken, however. His lawyers, who included counsel for Gould's Erie Railroad, found an obscure joker in the statutes with which an Appeals Court had to agree. No matter how many counts the indictment in Tweed's case contained, the maximum punishment could consist of only that prescribed for the first offense. So he was released in less than fourteen months, with his $12,750 fine reduced to $250; there is no record that he ever paid it.

But the law was not finished. As Tweed left his cell, he was arrested under a civil suit brought by the state to recover $6,000,000 in plunder that had been traced to him. Bail was set at $3,000,000 but Gould was afraid to furnish it this time. Tilden had become governor, and Gould didn't want a man with the White House on his mind going to work on his mottled affairs. So Tweed went to the Ludlow Street jail, whose erection had also stuffed his bank account.

But it was not a drab ten and a half months he spent there. He paid the warden well for the use of his official quarters and departed in a closed carriage each afternoon for the northern edge of the city, where he climbed out and took a long walk. On the way back he and the two keepers who accompanied him always stopped to enjoy a home-cooked dinner at his Fifth Avenue mansion.

The mansion, however, was getting to be all that the broken boss still owned. Counsel fees had staggered him and he was now being held as a debtor against the $6,000,000 judgment the state had won. That could go on indefinitely, which he did not propose to allow. So just before Christmas, 1875, during dinner at his home, Tweed remarked that he was going upstairs for a moment, then disappeared.

The last of his money took him to Cuba, and then to Spain. But less than a year after his escape, a Spanish sea-man identified him from a well-traveled Thomas Nast cartoon. He was returned to New York and the Ludlow Street jail, a beaten man with heart disease, shortly after Tilden was denied the U. S. presidency in the famous election contest against Rutherford B. Hayes.

Early in 1877, Tweed offered to tell all in the hope that he could finish out his life in freedom. He wrote to a state prosecutor:

I am an old man, greatly broken in health and cut down in spirits, and can no longer bear my burden . . . All further resistance being hopeless, I have none now to make and only seek the shortest and most efficient manner in which I can yield an unqualified surrender.

He told everything but he was not released. On April 12, 1877, a week after his fifty-fourth birthday, Tammany Hall's yard-armed pirate lay on a jail cot and gasped, "I have nothing left to settle except with my God. I know He will receive me."

Boss Tweed was dead.

CHAPTER VI

The Man Who Stomped the Devil

AS CAMP FOLLOWERS trail armies on
even the most sainted missions, religious
swindlers frequently infiltrate religion. Wearing an immunity conferred by our fear of interfering with sacred institutions, these marauders usually enjoy a mystically dictatorial hold on their followers.

Consider the "Leatherwood God," that huge, hallelujah-roaring faker who captured many of the Protestant churches of Ohio a century ago by proclaiming that he was God. The Leatherwood God was one of the first clearly insane fanatics to attach himself to religion in America. He was not a swindler, or at least he never succeeded in any swindlery; he was simply a lunatic who swindled himself and eventually drifted into obscurity.

And then there was Edmund Franz Creffield of Corvallis, Oregon, who raised as much hell as he warned against between 1903 and 1906. Creffield was more modest; he only claimed to be God's son. On the strength of that bewitching assertion, he enticed scores of Corvallis women into participating in rites more sexual than holy—rites that eventually led to his death at the hands of an outraged man. Creffield cannot properly be labeled a swindler either, since his motive was other than financial.

Only twenty years later, the people of the eastern seaboard of the United States were captivated by George Baker, a bald-headed little man who alleged he had been born in Providence—Providence, Heaven, that is. They watched his progress through twenty years, as he convinced disciples that the only God worth worshipping was himself. His banners were worded with stunning simplicity: FATHER DIVINE IS GOD ALMIGHTY.

The missing ingredient in all these wild-haired careers, the character streak whose absence kept all but the relatively recent Divine from retaining fame, was a dominant lust for big money. The man who successfully combines sanctimoniousness, sexual thievery, and the profit motive can be assured a place in the history of colorfully wasted lives. Such a man was hoary, pudgy, spindle-legged John Alexander Dowie—alias Elijah I, Elijah II, and Elijah the Restorer.

At the turn of the century John Dowie created a massive turmoil in the Midwest, invaded New York with 5,000 followers to stomp the devil and save the sinners, and spent or misspent twelve million dollars of the faithful's money before they sacked him in favor of an equally unbelievable leader.

Dowie's high-water mark was achieved when he fashioned an American Jerusalem on the shores of Lake Michigan that tolerated no foolishness from tourists and other infidels. Strangers who entered Zion, Illinois, were often read to from a *Handbook and Guide to Hell*, a casual hearing of which summarily reformed some and, it is said, drove others to laughter. The *Handbook* warned:

Every sinner is going to be punished with an overdose of his own sin. A tobacco smoker will be locked up in a den full of tobacco smoke. A chewer of the filthy weed will be immersed up to his neck in a vat of tobacco juice. A drinker will pass his time of purification in a natatorium filled with beer, wine and whiskey. Aye, Satan will care for those who smoke and drink in Zion.

As the visitors proceeded cautiously through the town, they were brought up short by a large, easily understood sign:

"Thieves and thugs will find this city hotter than Hell!"

John Alexander Dowie, the creator of all this brimstone, received an early psychological cue from his illiterate mother and pious, impoverished father. They, practitioners of straight-line religion, endowed him with the mental rigidity that stimulates quick, certain judgments and is blind to the color of gray. For the Dowies of Edinburgh, in 1847, all things were up or down, black or white, good or ghastly. With mankind immersed in sin, there was little room for temporizing with ids, egos, and emotional muddles.

This doctrine was applied to John, a frail, sickly child who was told to get strong forthwith. In 1860, when he was thirteen and the family emigrated to South Australia, he held firm religious precepts and vowed to become physically able to see them through. He lifted weights, stretched elastic bands, and ate like Bernarr Macfadden, all the while studying the Bible as if there were no tomorrow. He also turned a penny clerking in a grocery store in the port town of Adelaide.

The citizens of Adelaide unwittingly financed the first

matism and many other diseases," he proclaimed, and he spoke so authoritatively that those who abstained from pork constructed a syllogism of gratitude if not of logic. Since they didn't eat pork, they reasoned, they would not become sick, and not becoming sick was certainly as beneficial as being cured. So Dowie was indeed a healer.

Naturally, there were those whose ailments did not respond to mere mortal words, and such people had to be handled with care. "No one can be cured without faith," he told these unfortunates. "The fact that you are still ill shows you do not have enough faith. You must learn to believe." They went home and tried.

In six years, his blatherskite, plus a respectable record of curing hypochondriacs by giving them something to think about besides themselves, brought in enough money to broaden Dowie's outlook. He suggested that the Divine Healing Association become international and that he go off to spread the word globally. His followers proved so enthusiastic that they raised funds for this sainted mission. In June, 1888, after telling them he was bound for London, he landed in San Francisco, wicked hub of the Barbary Coast. Jane Dowie told John she thought she would like America.

As it turned out, Dowie would like it, too. He drifted for two years, seeking his bearings, and when he stopped in Chicago, it was to stay. He had never seen such sin in his life, nor so much need for divine healing. "I can get a good fight here with the Devil!" he said. He quickly sent word to numerous branches, which he had organized during his drifting, to begin sending their offerings to the new fount of healing. Then he erected a tent on the outskirts of town and set to work.

At first, the followers were attracted in small groups and Dowie did not press recruiting on any large scale. He preached just enough to hold the group together and to implant the notion that he should be offered tithes—one-tenth of their incomes. With these funds he traveled the back country of Illinois, Wisconsin, and Michigan, organizing more branches and biding his time. Aware that the Chicago World's Fair would open in 1893, he made several trips to the Jackson Park area and surveyed the real estate situation.

On opening day the resplendent main gate of the World's Fair was no more gaudy than a round wooden hut that stood just outside the grounds. Dowie arrived at the hut at seven A.M. and removed a piece of canvas that covered a red-lettered signboard reading: Zion Tabernacle. Then he sat on a camp stool before his own entrance and waited for his followers. At ten A.M., with the Fair grounds packed, he ordered an attack.

"Get them sinners in here!" he commanded.

His disciples purchased tickets and entered the World's Fair. Minutes later they began to return with men, women, and children in tow. As other minions snatched visitors from the Midway and the sideshows, Dowie invited the first customers into the tabernacle.

There he mounted a rostrum and preached faith healing. Passing through the audience, he laid hands on anyone and everyone, and soon they were discarding crutches and braces. Dowie collected these and used them to build a decoration behind his pulpit; they made a smashing exhibition for all the wondering crowds to see.

"These have been wrested from the Devil," he shrieked. "John Alexander Dowie has made the people walk again!"

The people inundated him with freewill offerings and he began preaching day and night, seven days a week, pausing only to regain strength. The susceptibles from among the Fair visitors packed his tabernacle. Money poured in from the branches and he sent converts even to the Far East to establish missions. By the beginning of 1895, contributions were arriving on an international basis.

At the same time, Dowie could not avoid a certain amount of legal difficulty. The medical profession was up in arms—less because of his violent attacks than because of his ability to dissuade people from seeking competent medical attention for progressing illnesses. Few doctors would deny that emotions and psyche played roles in therapy, but fewer still would consent to let Dowie administer the therapy.

The doctors' day came when some of Dowie's "patients" inevitably died. They demanded grand jury action and, as a result, Dowie referred to 1895 as "the year of persecution." He was arrested over one hundred times for violating ordinances regarding care of the ill. But not one night did he spend in jail. A battery of lawyers galloped about the courts with bail money and, through it all, he charged religious persecution. He spent about half the days of that year in courtrooms and, whenever he was convicted and fined, filed voluminous, complex appeals. He spent $20,000 on legal fees and court costs alone, but in the end he managed to overturn every conviction.

Naturally, he was becoming widely regarded as an underdog, and the fervence of his followers grew as their numbers and the indictments multiplied. He chose to ignore the few public debacles that occurred. In one, 3,000 medical students of the University of Chicago invited him to address them on "Doctors, Devils and Drugs." He smelled no rat, but when he arrived, he smelled dead cats with which the students had armed themselves, together with ill-smelling chemicals and stones. He needed a police escort to get back to his carriage.

Amid the laughter and the anger, Dowie moved steadily forward. He abandoned his shabby tabernacle and bought a seven-story building beside the handsome Illinois Central Railroad station on Michigan Avenue. There he and Jane set up luxurious housekeeping on the sixth and seventh floors. Followers became personal servants and the Dowies became plump, well-fed administrators. On Sundays he rented the Chicago Auditorium and spoke to thousands, telling them that a major development in the crusade was imminent. While they waited, they put their money into his newly established Zion City Bank, on the ground floor of his Michigan Avenue Heaven.

Suddenly the healer's weekdays became mysterious. He disappeared early each morning, telling no one his destination, and returned late at night, chuckling with a strange satisfaction. One night he showed Jane a document that declared him sole stockholder of a company known as the Zion Land and Investment Association. Jane was not the only one who was mystified by this firm. Real estate operators in Benton township on Lake Michigan, halfway between Chicago and Milwaukee, were baffled by a peculiar activity in usually slow-moving land parcels they were offering. Before they could establish a pattern and inflate the prices, Dowie had bought 6,500 acres—over ten square miles of some of the most beautiful land in Illinois—for less than $200 an acre, or a total of $1,250,000. Without his crafty furtiveness, he would have paid that much just for the two-and-a-half-mile strip that lay directly on the lake.

With this land in hand, Dowie was ready for the first of three major announcements. One Sunday in January, 1899, he announced to 5,000 persons in Chicago Auditorium that he was founding the "Christian Catholic Church in Zion," J. A. Dowie, General Overseer. All branches of the International Divine Healing Association would automatically become Churches of Zion. In the entire transition, despite some wavering by less spirited enthusiasts, he did not lose a single faith healing branch.

Dowie then decided to visit his missions in Europe, to stimulate their activities. After a rapid inspection tour, he spent the balance of his time in Nottingham, England, which was the site of a prosperous lace factory. Lace was not manufactured in the United States and was being imported under a sixty percent tariff, which made it an attractive business, if one could be in it in America. Dowie bought the factory and arranged for its machinery and equipment to be sent to Illinois, together with technicians, when he called for them.

All was ready now for his triumphant return to the Chicago rostrum. On the first Sunday after his arrival he made his second major announcement. He strode to the pulpit on his bandy legs and trained his beady eyes on the assemblage. Then he delivered the decree that was to establish the most peculiar city in the annals of American settlements.

"We are going to leave sinful Chicago," he declared, "and form our own metropolis. On the shores of Lake Michigan, in the city of Zion, we will live as God intended, without the corruption of tobacco, whiskey and the other stinkpots of the sinners."

The faithful went wild, and plans for the Twentieth Century Exodus went forward.

Now Dowie was ready for his most important declaration. A great man for detail, he waited until all preparations had been made by his pioneers. Then, on June 2, 1901, he took his place in the ranks of gigantic religious swindlers.

Before 7,000 people, he proclaimed himself the reincarnation of the Prophet Elijah, and said that those who came with him to his Zion would not be able to challenge his authority, which would be the same as God's. The idea of having such direct access to the Lord overwhelmed his audience, and they went along almost to a man, although some intramural disputes did break out. Some insisted on calling him Elijah II, while others called him Elijah III, declaring that John the Baptist had been Elijah II. As for Dowie, he was not one to allow such pettifogging wrangles to disrupt his plans; he side-stepped the issue by simply calling himself Elijah the Restorer. The important thing, he said, was his mission to prepare earth for the return of Christ. Therefore, he would live until that day came, regardless of the condition of the flesh. And, he added, he would do it without those grubbing doctors.

Dowie was not so foolish as to think he did not need a rationale for his earth-shaking assumption of Elijah's mantle. Using the first person plural to refer to himself, he asked, "How do we know we are Elijah the Restorer?" Then he replied, "We know this because it has been imposed on us by God Himself. Had we been deceived in this matter, then God would have deceived us. That is an impossibility." The logic, like the man's gall, was almost indestructible.

The thesis did come under some attack, however. Orthodox ministers and newspaper editors howled in outrage and scorn. But Dowie replied without retreat: "I *am* Elijah. I say it fearlessly. Make the most of it, you wretches in ecclesiastical garb!" He raged at the Masons, the Pope, the bankers, and the press. "You talk about your democracy," he said. "Bah! I tell you democracy has been tried in the balance and has failed."

When doctors commented that he sounded paranoid, he charged that they were plotting to kidnap him, lock him in a detention hospital, "and beat me on the head until I am insane." He picked up his belongings, entered a carriage, and was driven to the New Jerusalem. Five thousand Zionites followed, by whatever transportation they could muster.

Everyone turned out to build a temporary shelter for the Grand Overseer, and they placed it just down the road from the Chicago and Northwestern Railway station, on Elijah Avenue. After constructing wooden houses for themselves, they found a choice spot in the bluish mud of the lake shore and built a permanent structure worthy of their leader—an ornate, three story mansion which was christened Shiloh House. For some reason never explained, Elijah ordered its roof painted with red, yellow, and green zig-zagging stripes.

The lace factory arrived in parts and was made whole. Its technicians appeared and soon the machines were humming over eight acres of floor space. Up went a bank, a publishing house, a tabernacle to seat 7,000, a brickworks (capacity: 40,000 bricks a day), a college, and a Home of Hope for Erring Women (Jane Dowie, Overseer, in charge). A real estate company parceled out all homesites and wrote the deeds, which were strange as land transactions go. Under their terms, every grain of soil in Zion belonged to Elijah, and buyers merely rented under leases that would expire in 3000 A.D. As Grand Overseer he owned the bank, factories, tabernacle, and everything else from shoes to souls. Missionaries in the Caribbean, Australia, and the Far East were sending in $1,000 a day and there was no accounting of tithes, profits, or anything else. By the end of 1901, Chicago financial circles grudgingly conceded that the Prophet's assets has passed the $5,000,000 mark.

This tremendous activity proved a severe drain on even a prophet's time and energy, and Dowie found that while he had increasingly less time in which to pray, he was getting increasingly more requests for spiritual help. Declining to overlook even the most frivolous request, he installed a time-stamping machine and handled the prayer requests in omnibus fashion. As requests were received, they were stamped, "Prayed May 10, three P.M. John A. Dowie," and in the evening, when he could catch his breath, he prayed for everyone in one catch-all meditation. It was, if spiritually deficient, practically efficient.

Through all these years of religio-merchandising, Dowie had been raising a family, like other mortals. He had a son, John Alexander Gladstone Dowie, who, he proudly announced, had never been kissed by a girl, and who was consequently referred to in the newspapers as "Gladstone the Unkissed," and he had a daughter, Esther, an embarrassed student at the University of Chicago. John and Jane tried to inculcate their children with their own soap opera brand of godliness, but Gladstone seemed to take more to it than Esther. She was a little too worldly; she even read books about heretic non-Dowie forms of religion.

Nevertheless, she was her father's favorite, and he was horrified to be told one morning that she had been seriously burned in her dormitory room at the University. A breeze had blown her nightgown into a lamp flame and she was burned over her entire body. Dowie hurried down to Chicago and found that one of his followers (who, strangely enough, was also a practicing physician) had tried to ease her pain by covering her body with vaseline. After banishing the doctor from the Christian Catholic Church for invoking such pagan measures, he went to Esther's bedside and found her delirious with pain. Refusing to allow any medical treatment, he prayed at her side all day. At nine o'clock that evening the girl died in agony. The Prophet returned to Zion with an explanation that astounded non-believers and chilled his flock.

"She died," he said, "because she ignored my injunction against employing alcohol in any form." Esther had used alcohol in the lamp whose flames had burned her.

At Dowie's side to console him was a man who had come to Zion from a brimstone-hellfire of his own, and who, if Dowie but knew it, would one day give the Grand Overseer a hard time. He was Wilbur Glenn Voliva, an Indiana fundamentalist preacher who was to delight the public by declaring, "I can whip to smithereens any man in the world in a mental battle. I have never met any professor or student who knew a millionth as much on any subject as I do."

Voliva had embraced Dowieism after reading one of

Elijah's pungent periodicals, *Leaves of Healing*. When he presented himself at Zion, Dowie promptly made him an elder of the church. Voliva so ingratiated himself with the tithe-paying citizens of Zion that Dowie grew fearful; despite the disciple's solicitude, he sent him off to Australia that summer to carry the Word down under, far away.

With Voliva's real or imagined threat disposed of in mid-1902, the Prophet applied himself to consolidating his grasp on Zion. He arranged for the creation of a bakery, and soap, candy, and biscuit factories. Then he set up the Theocratic Party and declared it to be the official party of the Christian Catholic Church. Other parties could form in Zion, but it was clear that organizing them would be a monumental waste of time. From the first no-contest election forward, Dowie named Zion's mayor and all other officials.

He also promulgated blue laws that not even the Puritans had thought of. The Municipal Code of Zion provided that all persons must extinguish cigarettes, cigars, or pipes when requested to do so by anyone standing within five feet. It also proscribed establishment of any business. And Section 795 declared: "It shall be unlawful for any person, firm or corporation to engage in the sale at retail of tobacco in any form." Also outlawed were dancing, movies, theaters, circuses, carnivals, and sporting events.

To enforce these laws, and be personally loyal to him, Dowie formed an 800-man Zion Guard, which he armed and dressed in para-military uniforms on which the good women of Zion embroidered figures of doves. Bibles hung from the guards' belts and the word *Patience* appeared in gold lace on their caps. One of their standing orders was to swoop down on women whose necks were bare, and

cover them with woolen shawls. Sex would not run ram-
pant in Zion.

But sex for the citizens and sex for Elijah were different
matters. At fifty-five, despite his large middle and spindly
extremities, Dowie considered himself a dashing figure, and,
for him, sex was not to be considered sinful. Accordingly,
he adopted the practice of holding night meetings at which
special religious instructions were given to women only.
Sometimes, while Jane Dowie labored on at the Home of
Hope for Erring Women, he transported a troupe of
ladies to his $200,000 summer mansion in Michigan. But
usually they met at Shiloh House, which was a place of
deceptive architecture. On the second floor, at the back,
was a room that could be reached only through two steel
doors. Its tiny window was closed and barred, and the
room was ventilated by a pipe that led outside. The sole
piece of furniture was a large bed in the center of the
floor, and the bed was as odd as the room. Wires led from
hidden batteries through the mattress and springs, and
while no woman of Zion ever revealed the bed's secrets,
they all said it was nothing short of marvelous.

Under the circumstances, the marvel lay in the fact that
Elijah wasn't carried out of town on a rail. As a matter of
fact, gossipy mumblings and rumblings did come to his
ear in early 1903, whereupon he decided that Zion needed
a first-class diversion. Less than 1,000 miles to the east was
one of the most sinful diversions to be found—New York
City, with its cabarets, theatrical women, smoking, drinking and swearing men, high-priced doctors, gambling, and
laggard church attendance. One Sunday Elijah mounted
his pulpit, cried without letup, and told the Zionites they
were going to descend on New York as an army and

snatch the sinners from the grip of the devil. "You will bring the people to Madison Square Garden," he said, "and I will dynamite them!"

Whatever weapons he chose, he would be able to afford them. His thoroughgoing extraction of funds from his followers had by then put $23,000,000 at his disposal.

Dowie rented old Madison Square Garden, in lower Manhattan, for two weeks in October, but preparations to receive his crusade began in midsummer with an invasion of New York by an advance guard from Zion. Elders, entrusted with culinary, lodging, and other problems, swarmed the city, lining up rooms for the faithful. Elijah took care of his own accommodations, reserving a grand suite at the Plaza, overlooking Central Park. For weeks before the Crusade opened, Dowieites were surveying the interior of the Garden to lay out their cooking and serving facilities.

On Wednesday, October 13, 1903, the first train was loaded at Zion. All was well organized. The 500-voice Zion Choir lined up at the railroad station, sang two hymns, then boarded the coaches in an orderly manner. Two days later eight trains had left, the last one carrying a car that belonged to the president of the Nickel Plate Railroad. In it sat Dowie, Jane, and "The Unkissed One." Their own horses and carriage filled a freight car, and thirty-eight trunks and suitcases clogged a baggage car.

On Saturday morning, when the Prophet arrived in Grand Central Station, he entered upon a two-week devotional circus that has not been equalled in New York to this day. An embarrassing incident developed immediately when, somewhere in the station, plain Jane Dowie was robbed of a diamond-and-pearl brooch. When the Prophet heard that the figure $1,500 was being bandied about, he denied she even owned such an ostentatious bauble, let alone was robbed of it. Jane withdrew her complaint and they rode off to the Plaza.

That afternoon they visited the Garden, where Dowie prepared his followers before they set out to knock on every door in Manhattan. The city had been divided into districts, and the Dowieites organized as leaders, captains, and bellringers. He warned them not to argue with apartment house superintendents, who, he said, were as surly as the man-eating concierges of Paris. While a thirty-man fife and drum corps played, the faithful marched off in all directions to save the city.

On opening night, Tuesday, Dowie, his followers, 12,000 curious New Yorkers, and the devil arrived at the Garden almost simultaneously. The Zion Choir sang as seats were taken, and then the Dowies appeared at a stairway that led to a speaker's platform. Elijah wore the robes of a bishop, with big, white balloon sleeves that puffed as he climbed with measured step to his place. Behind him came Jane, gentle, sad-eyed, and also in bishop's robes. "The Unkissed One," clad in the purple of an archbishop, brought up the rear.

Dowie signaled the white-gowned choir to desist, then came forward under a spotlight and stared at the crowd, his round pink face framed by long white hair and shaggy beard. Bushy black eyebrows completed the picture of a commanding figure.

"It looked," wrote a reporter for the New York *American*, "as if this man was going to win."

But then he spoke, and that was John Dowie's error. He

had been accustomed to smaller settings, in which his strong voice dominated. But now he was in the massive Garden, and the charmed tones suddenly sounded shrill, metallic, and grating. His delivery was scolding, even bullying.

"This city is a stinkpot!" he shouted. "This is a house of sin. You New Yorkers belong to the Devil, and he will lead you to Hell! Change your ways, I say, before the fires engulf you!"

On and on he went, his fervor rising by the sentence. Drunk with power, his judgment diluted by blind adulation, he had measured his audience with the wrong yardstick. At first by two's and three's, then in larger groups, the crowd rose and moved to the exits. Some were yawning. Dowie's body suddenly shook with rage.

"Sit down!" he screamed. "You *must* sit down. You shall not go out!"

Few people even looked back. He pulled at his beard and tore out some long whiskers. He called to his Zion Guards, "Stop those people! Captain of the Zion Guard, I command you not to let one of them go out!" The captain drew up his Bible-toting guardsmen in a thin blue line and tried to cover the exits, but by then the ranks of the departers had so swelled that they carried the Guards out into Madison Avenue with them. Dowie railed on, but soon half his audience was gone, and then two-thirds succumbed to the devil.

That evening he told his followers the salvation of New York would be even more difficult than he had expected.

The following night he opened to a crowd of 6,000, but before he had billingsgated five minutes, a bony figure of a woman rose from the audience and interrupted. He out-shouted her, but she remained on her feet. It was Carrie Nation, whom few men could claim to have squelched. The Zion Guards finally encircled her and hustled her outside, but the damage had been done; two-thirds of the audience followed.

On Wednesday night the disorder bordered on riot and Dowie gave up after five minutes. On and on it went, each night a more miserable debacle than the previous, and finally the morbid sideshow ended with the baptism of fifty converts in a tank thirty feet square. Their souls had been saved at a cost of $500,000, or $10,000 apiece, which stood, for over fifty years, as the highest price ever spent for evangelical conversions.

Now the trouble began in earnest. Process servers hounded Dowie for unpaid bills and found him short of cash. Hastily, he took Jane and young Gladstone up to Boston and put them on a boat for Australia. Then he went down to Washington where, for a reason that evades explanation, Theodore Roosevelt received him in the White House and chatted almost an hour. Finally, with some apprehension, Dowie returned to Zion.

Taking stock, he faced an awful truth. Between his expensive soul-saving crusade, his opulent life, and his mismanagement of Zion's industries, the town was in staggering financial trouble. When he closed down the candy factory, murmurs of discontent arose, and so did the fear in his heart. He tried desperately for a year to recoup, but conditions grew bleaker. What Zion needed, it was clear, was still another diversion.

His back to the wall, the Prophet delivered an epic announcement. He was off to Mexico, he said, to establish a huge branch of the church on a site to be called "Paradise Plantation." Then would come formation of another Jerusalem, this time in Africa, on the Nile. Excitement mounted once more, perhaps not so high as on previous occasions, but high enough. Now he had to find someone to replace him while he was in Mexico, and here he faced a difficulty he had fashioned himself. His iron grip on the town's affairs had precluded development of anyone with leadership ability or administrative knowledge. So he was led, despite his earlier qualms, to Wilbur Glenn Voliva, and he ordered him to return from Australia at once.

Then the Prophet attacked one remaining problem. He interviewed scores of female Zionites to see which of them would win the honor of accompanying him—without their husbands. When he had chosen a dozen and had turned over a power of attorney to Voliva, he and his women followed the birds south to Monterrey. Wife Jane, who had returned from Australia with "The Unkissed One," stayed behind.

Like the embezzling bank teller who takes a vacation and lets prying eyes inspect his books, Dowie should never have left the store. Almost from the moment he departed, the men whose wives had accompanied him began to wag tongues. Others joined and soon a couple of wives divulged the nature of the all night services the Prophet had conducted.

One night a group of discontented men entered Shiloh House and battered their way into the secret room that contained the electrified bed. They also found a vast collection of smutty literature. And finally, they discovered hanging in a closet a battery set which, they surmised, provided the current for his electrified bed therapy.

On the economic front, even worse shenanigans came to light. Wilbur Voliva hadn't had access to Zion's accounts for sixty days before he shrieked in financial horror. Dowie had gambled in the stock market during the 1903 slump and lost $1,200,000. Zion Industries was bankrupt. The old man had milked it of millions and left the companies' structures little more than hollow shells.

In April, 1906, despite the fact that he heard Dowie had suffered a stroke and gone to Jamaica to recuperate, Voliva called a meeting of the elders and charged the Prophet with mismanagement of funds, immorality, and the endorsement of polygamy. During a five-hour hearing, wife Jane took the stand and shocked the elders by revealing that Dowie had asked her for a divorce the previous fall. He planned a seven-wife harem, she said, and had already proposed to five women and been accepted. The elders unanimously repudiated the old man, and a meeting of all the faithful took the same step almost without dissent. Voliva, using his power of attorney, immediately took title to everything in Zion.

Now this was a drastic move indeed against God's special helper, and Dowie took the news poorly. Crying vengeance, he hurried home with his women, whose husbands promptly beat them and locked them up at home. The Prophet went to Federal Court in Chicago and asked Judge Kenesaw Mountain Landis to make Voliva give him back his city. Landis was colorful, as everyone knows, but he wasn't *that* colorful, and he threw Dowie out of court. At the same time he declared Zion bankrupt and put its affairs into the hands of a receiver.

The crushed faker hurried back to Zion, where Jane told him she was through; his son Gladstone wouldn't even speak to him. He preached, but few would listen. When those who did come cursed him as a betrayer, he lost control and tore at his clothing and his beard, both of which gave way. Then he retired to Shiloh House, where he lay on his bed for six months, quite out of his mind, until one morning in March, 1907.

On that day he awoke and muttered, "Joy to the world, the Lord has come!" Apparently feeling it was therefore safe to die, he died, at the age of fifty-nine.

After the financial and emotional beating Zion took from John Alexander Dowie, it deserved a period of rational peace. That is not what it got from ponderous, paunchy Wilbur Glenn Voliva who, in his own way, was even less sane than his predecessor. One of his first public statements pointed out that the earth is flat and motionless, and that the sun is not 91,000,000 miles away, but only 3,000 miles distant. "If you wanted to light up Chicago," he asked, "would you put your light in San Francisco?"

But before Voliva could devote his full attention to such notions, he had to save Zion from the devil, or receiver, which were considered to be the same thing. And he did. After losing several court battles with creditors, he left town with eighty-seven cents and set up a tent on the outskirts. There he harangued the remnants of the faithful and raised $3,500 at his first meeting. "The day will come," he declared, "when I will own every foot, every inch and every pinch of the city of Zion." It seems incredible that the citizens would buy that approach again, but they did. Factory by factory, Voliva regained control, until finally he received every deed in Zion for a total cost of $200,000. Soon he was active head of twenty resuscitated institutions and industries, which did an annual business of over $5,000,000 exclusive of real estate transactions.

Just as fundamentalist as Dowie, he sat in a great chair at a massive table in Shiloh House and decreed heavy fines for smokers, swearers, and Sunday whistlers. He wore a Prince Albert and a quilted cravat and, all in all, cut a comical figure. When he persisted in his contention that the earth was as flat as a flapjack, and Arthur Brisbane called him "an ass to be pitied," he stormed: "Every man who fights me goes under. Mark what I say! The grave-yard is full of fellows who tried to down Voliva. God Almighty smites them!"

In 1915 his wife died after he had prevented her from receiving medical assistance. He himself died in 1942, after promising that he would live to one hundred and twenty on Brazil nuts and buttermilk.

As for Zion, the old timers wouldn't know it today. There is as much fingernail polish in the town as anywhere else, and whistling is no longer subversive. The Theocratic Party is gone, the Tabernacle burned down in 1937, and for a number of years the profits of some of Zion's industries went to New York University, an institution that probably thinks the earth is round.

All of which is not to say that the last traces of Dowie-ism have evaporated. In Zion there still live a handful of aged people who, bewilderedly, remember their departed leaders and wonder what has happened. They wouldn't agree with the 1907 observer who said of John Alexander Dowie, "He was a faker, was Dowie, but let no man say he was a little faker."

CHAPTER VII

The Prophet Who Profited

ROBERT MATTHEWS was born in 1788, only a year before the Bill of Rights was adopted with its injunction that no law should interfere with religious institutions. Matthews grew up to establish his own religion—a religion so outrageous in its rites that the law was forced to interfere with it.

During the decade following 1825, Matthews operated as the first flamboyant religious swindler to afflict the United States. He made a screwball brand of worship the most lucrative and depraved in the new nation. At one time he claimed to be the Prophet Matthias, who replaced Judas after the betrayal of Christ, and at another he claimed to be God on earth.

But at all times, regardless of the claim of the moment, he was a prophet who profited.

In upstate New York, where he was born, Robert Matthews was attracting awe by the time he was eight years old. It was then that he first claimed the most supernatural of powers, a claim he used to extort candy from his schoolmates. He glared at the lowering sky and said he would make the man in the clouds roar with anger. When a resounding peal of thunder frightened the boys into giving up their sweets, they asked Matthews if he knew the man in the clouds.

"Why, yes," he replied. "He's my uncle."

By the time he was sixteen, he was being referred to as "Jumping Jesus"—not because the spirit of the antichrist dominated the new nation, but because of his cloying evangelism and vexing pretensions. He was considering becoming a carpenter, he explained, because that was what Jesus had done.

Soon afterward he left home to preach. Allowing his prematurely white hair to grow to his shoulders and his curly beard to descend to his navel, he stumped revival meetings through the rural areas of the state and flayed the use of alcohol, tobacco, and meat. These were not personal dislikes, he pointed out. It was simply that God had asked him to cleanse the earth and reestablish primitive peacefulness, and he would not be able to do that if the current inhabitants ate the animals, for example.

Since temperance and vegetarianism were well-regarded backwoods causes, his following gradually swelled. By 1820, when he enjoyed a scattered but devoted following, it was but a modest leap to the impossibly fanatic. He felt an uplifting twinge of immortality and asserted that he had been reborn. Henceforth, he announced, he was not Matthews, but the Prophet Matthias.

Six years later, when the Prophet was thirty-eight and had taken unto himself a wife, he scented a major opportunity for expansion of his divine role. It was 1826, and a piece of political Americana was being enacted in the town of Batavia, not far from what was about to be incorporated as Buffalo.

During a warm election contest, in which the issue of freemasonry was providing a rather reddish herring for politicians, a mechanic named William Morgan disappeared. Because Morgan was a former Mason who had been accused of divulging the order's secrets, a cry of murder was raised against the fraternity. The public was properly outraged and, when a body was found and identified as Morgan's, legend has it that a naive anti-Mason questioned the authenticity of the identification. A companion quickly silenced him with an observation heard in one form or another to this day. "A good enough Morgan until after the election," the more practical man said. He then proceeded to word-whip the Masons into the role of assassins—a characterization they were relieved of only when the votes had been cast.

Matthews realized that Mason-hating was a popular drawing card, and when he heard that the society was being taxed with Morgan's death, he hurried to Batavia astride the fastest mule a poor man could afford. Once there, he filched some strips of clothing from the body of whoever the dead man was and, with these, began riding the circuit of camp meetings in the western counties of New York State.

At the first revival, displaying the clothing in the "I hold here in my hand" manner, he announced that God had bade him "dissolve" the Masonic Order and that, therefore, it no longer existed. At the next camp he dissolved *all* secret organizations, including grand juries. Some weeks later, when he was winding up his tour—having left a distinct impression on the impressionable from Niagara Falls

east to Albany—he took his fateful step, one he had
prepared for by refusing to identify himself with any
particular religious denomination.

"I am Matthias!" he declared. "Matthias the Prophet!"
Later he added that he was the earthly personification of
God. His deep-set eyes shone beneath bushy eyebrows,
his beard wagged, and his mane fluttered across his shoulders as he reached for infinity.

People believed him—or, at least, enough people believed him to make the project a worthwhile investment.
So, abandoning his wife and three children, he went down
to New York City to find a wealthy businessman who had
been described as a most devout person. Matthias was not
to be the apostle of the poor.

The merchant, Sylvester Mills, proved that an affluent
man could be as credulous as a pauper. He had heard of
Matthias and longed to meet him; almost from the moment
the imposing fake strode into his store on Pearl Street, the
cultivated, well-educated Mills was converted. Matthias
left his camp-meeting manners behind and conducted himself in a forceful but dignified manner. He asserted his
divinity once again, and when Mills mildly questioned it,
he declined to argue the matter; that was the way things
were, he said very courteously. Take it or leave it.

Mills, after some puzzlement, took it. He invited Matthias to his home where, over the next few weeks, he
listened while Matthias talked. At the end of that period
the reborn prophet owned the merchant's mind and
money. As Prophet Dowie did later, he declared he would
never die. Instead, from his seat of power, the New
Jerusalem which would soon come floating down from
Heaven, he would rule the earth as God alive.

Since his was to be a spiritual reign, Matthias could not be expected to continue in common clothes. Mills agreed, and supplied money and a bewildered haberdasher. Soon Matthias appeared in his version of immortal raiment. Around his neck hung a massive key of solid gold, to symbolize his power over the gates of the new city. He carried a six-foot graduated rod with which he would lay out its dimensions, and from a wide leather belt hung a keen, two-edged sword. Woven into a silk blouse were stars, moons, and crowns, and a sun of blazing gold adorned a black velvet cap. The finishing touches were provided by white kid gloves, his flowing locks, and his awesome beard. He was an incarnate buffoon, except to Mills.

Matthias made Mills' home his own and from it he preached to a select group of the merchant's friends. He taught them the importance of baptism by immersion, followed by circumcision, and performed both rites himself on some of Mills' friends.

Sylvester Mills' relatives, however, were not believers. They became so distressed at the merchant's state of mind, and the state of his dwindling fortune, that his wife arranged for a legal examination of the man's mind; whereupon he was committed to an asylum and Matthias to the city jail as a vagrant and imposter. When he roared at the police officers and promised them an early death, they fearlessly flung him into a cell.

But confinement was brief for both. The pre-Freudian doctors, who examined Mills, found no evidence of lunacy except a warped approach to religion. So he was released, which made it impossible to keep Matthias under lock and key. Together, the happy pair returned to Mills' home, where the crusade was renewed with increased vigor. Mills, however, was only human, and when his relatives sent a lawyer around to explain that they would have him put away every two months unless he stopped his foolishness, his fervor abated. He ordered Matthias to leave, but softened the blow by introducing the master to another man of means. Since Mills' fortune was rapidly running out, Matthias was unperturbed.

The new disciple was Elijah Pierson, an elderly gentleman who was about to retire from business with $70,000 to see him through his dotage. Pierson was so convinced that prayer produced miracles that, when his wife died, he prayed that she be brought back from the dead. And, like the Biblical Elijah, he stretched his body over hers. When she failed to respond, the morticians buried her, over his protests.

Shortly after this melancholy incident, Matthias arrived at Pierson's home, thirty miles above New York City in what was then called Sing Sing but later became Ossining because the association with the penal institution was too much for queasy residents. Pierson's maid answered Matthias' knock and when she saw his remarkable costume she asked, "Are you Christ?"

"I am," he replied.

The maid fainted and Pierson had to come to the door himself.

With Pierson at the time was another rich Sing Singer, Benjamin Folger, and Matthias lost no time in knighting both. Henceforth, Pierson would be Prophet Elijah and Folger, John the Baptist. Matthias visited Folger's home, found it superior to Pierson's, and had it signed over to him within a month. The followers also inventoried their entire fortunes and turned these over. The leader was so grateful that he invited Pierson and Mr. and Mrs. Folger to live with him in his new home. They agreed.

It was here in the rustic splendor of Westchester County that the swindler hit his stride. Like other religious extremists who preceded and followed him, he made a lascivious right of sex. As a prelude, he established a method of prayer in which all hands prostrated themselves in a circle around him. There they learned to pray to him with gusto; when this was lacking, he railed and threatened not to save them from the earthly disaster that was coming. Then he sermonized on marriage.

"Wedlock," he said, "is a heathenish institution. Sexual practices must be returned to simplicity. Marriage will be abolished." This led to a ceremony called "Purification From Marriage," in which everyone lay naked on the floor as he washed their bodies with a sponge and made them "virgins of the garden."

Then came the coup. The pompous fake summoned Folger one day and announced that he was ready to begin populating the earth with new, divine souls. They would be produced through mortal methods—but still, they would be divine. The reason? Matthias himself would provide the first seed. And Folger's wife would mother the first male of the new generation. If Folger was disturbed by this arrangement, he did not show it.

To keep Folger's time from hanging heavily on his hands during this process, Matthias honored him, too. Folger would father the first new female. The mother would be one of Matthias' own daughters, whom he had kept track of during the seven years since he abandoned the family. She lived in Albany, which was not far, and she was married, which was not an obstacle, he said.

As for creaky old Pierson, he was sent outside to garden.

Matthias' daughter, Isabella, who strangely enough retained some affection for him, was married to an Albany combmaker named Charles Laisdell. She had just turned eighteen when Matthias moved the willing Mrs. Folger into his own bedroom and sent for her. Before she had even unpacked, Mrs. Folger was inculcating her in the way sexual matters were handled around the house. Isabella was shocked, and when Mrs. Folger told her that Mr. Folger awaited her in his bedroom and that her mission was to produce a divine child with him, she slapped the addled woman and locked herself in a bedroom—not Mr. Folger's.

Mrs. Folger angrily hurried to the master and denounced his heretic daughter. Together, they prayed for Isabella's soul, and then Matthias sent for her. All the literal hell he conjured would not shake her determination to have no part of this rite, and so he flogged her insensible with a raw cowhide. She was placed in bed and prayed for again, and the next day was examined to see if she had succeeded in getting religion. She hadn't, and Matthias beat her so severely this time that she was unable to leave her bed for weeks.

Isabella's comb-making husband wrote several letters to his wife, but received no replies; Matthias simply fed the correspondence to the fireplace. Worried, Laisdell journeyed to Sing Sing but Matthias' servants held him off while the Prophet and the Folgers packed Isabella off to a New York City house that Pierson had donated to the cause. When Laisdell finally forced his way in, Pierson tried to make him see things Matthias' way. Laisdell staggered the old gentleman with a righteous blow and called the police.

By next morning Matthias' carriage was traced to the town house, whose door was opened by the richly robed one himself when Laisdell and three officers pounded on it. Laisdell demanded his wife. Matthias said Laisdell had no wife; the marriage was illegal because he had not performed the ceremony. Laisdell demanded the woman named Isabella, wife or no. Matthias drew his two-edged sword and barred the way. The police pushed him aside and Laisdell rushed inside; he was hysterical by the time he arranged for a carriage to take Isabella and him posthaste to Albany. As for Matthias, he was not arrested because, the police explained, he was, after all, Isabella's father.

The Prophet, who still owed Folger a wife, explained that God suffered occasional setbacks while establishing His reign over earth, and that they had just lived through one. Folger was generously understanding. In his spare time, he had converted a pretty young housewife to the new religion, and he said he would settle for her. Matthias explained to her how lucky she was and dispatched her to Folger immediately. The troupe retired to Westchester once more—Matthias in possession of Mrs. Folger—and all debts were squared.

There were two months yet before Mrs. Folger was due to deliver the first divine male and, in that time, Matthias added one more tenet to his creed. He announced that during this period he would freely take as his wife the seven other women who, by then, made up the holy household. He would have one for each day of the week, so no other male would be deprived more than one night.

The sky fell in on roguish Matthias the day Mrs. Folger gave birth. He had played a fifty-fifty chance that the child's sex would be male, and he lost. It was a girl. The followers were dismayed, and the most shaken was Folger. His faith broke and he served notice that he wanted his house and money back within three months.

Pierson came in out of the garden and discordantly demanded his $70,000 back, without three months' grace. So Matthias picked some special blackberries for the old man and had him to tea. The following morning Pierson became ill and six days later died in agony. Matthias said he had died of pneumonia and buried him without notifying the Westchester County authorities.

On the day before the deadline Folger had set for the return of his home and fortune, Matthias awoke early and, thoughtful soul, prepared coffee for the household. As they all sat down to breakfast he arose and said he would take a carriage ride to get rid of a headache. As he left, the Folgers tasted their coffee and found it vile. They took no more than a sip and both became ill immediately. They were sick all day, during which time their high priest did not return. That evening Folger, now in a raging suspicion, called the police and suggested the departed Mr. Pierson's body be examined for evidence of poison. It was, and his liver was found full of arsenic.

Matthias, apprehended in Albany, was returned to Westchester County on a murder indictment. This revelation so revolted his daughter Isabella that she decided to report her floggings. Another indictment came down.

In April, 1835, the sanctimonious fake was brought to court in White Plains to stand trial. He demanded that he first be allowed to address his dwindled core of followers. He walked out into the center of a graveyard that was walled in on all sides by high rocks. Pointing his rod at the sky, he shouted, "I shall make these walls fall!"

A wall fell. The court attendants were so alarmed they almost set him free, but then four boys came in and confessed they had been pushing the rocks from a bluff above the graveyard; they had caused a landslide. At least, that's what *they* said. Matthias and his tiny flock were convinced otherwise.

When the wall-wrecker faced the judge, he had an announcement to make that, he said, would stop the trial before it started. "I speak in reference to the proceedings of the grand jury," he declared. "It is a secret institution and I hereby proclaim that all secret societies are dissolved. As a matter of fact, I dissolved them years ago. They have the curse of Almighty God on them and they are dissolved!" The judge let him scream "dissolved" thirty times, then turned him over to a panel of doctors who found this insane man sane, and said he should stand trial.

And so he did. But they couldn't hang murder on him, despite the evidence of arsenic in Elijah Pierson's cadaver. When the jury brought in its verdict, the foreman said they had not found enough direct evidence to convict, and added, "But must we acquit him? Must we?" Sadly, the judge said they must.

Next came the trial for flogging Isabella, again on an indictment handed down by a secret institution. This time Matthias was found guilty and sentenced to three months in jail, plus another month for contempt of court. He got a day in prison for every time he had shouted, "Dissolved!"

Mills' and Folger's fortunes were dissipated, Mrs. Folger suffered a mental collapse, only $7,000 was recovered of Pierson's $70,000, and Matthias promised he would kill all parties concerned the moment he was free. But upon his release he vanished and was not seen again. For all anyone knows, he might have started out for Heaven and lost his way.

CHAPTER VIII

A Case of Salted Diamonds

JUST WHEN most people decide that, with the possible exception of oil, most of the world's natural treasures have been located, someone proves that each new dawning provides fresh hope and opportunity.

That happened on an October afternoon in 1956, when two South African scientists were ambling through the Mweza Hills of Southern Rhodesia. They were searching for a mineral that performs some mundane task in the hardening of iron and copper. As they happened onto a clearing the size of a suburban development backyard, the scientists decided to evade the punishing African sun under a stunted tree. There they became wealthy, for they stumbled onto emeralds; so many of the bright green stones that they scooped them up in their hands. Experts have described the gems as the most beautifully colored the world has ever seen, and the scientists, at last report, were rejecting offers of three million dollars for a one-fourth interest in their discovery.

The most engaging aspect of the story is that it is true. Nobody swindled anybody. Nobody planted emeralds in the African soil so he could reap a fortune from enchanted investors. Nobody was dishonest and nothing was crooked.

The same sort of discovery occurred a number of years ago in the wild West of the United States, with one compelling exception. This discovery *was* a swindle, and enchanted investors did get taken in. People *were* dishonest, and everything *was* crooked.

In the early days of February, 1872, San Franciscans excitedly received news of the greatest find since the gold dust of '49. Somewhere in the West, someone had stumbled onto an entire mountain of diamonds. Imagine, a whole mountain! No one knew exactly where, but they all knew it was real.

The bearers of this astonishing news looked exactly as they should. John Slack and Philip Arnold were their names, and they were grizzled sourdoughs with proper mats of beard and the dust of the hill trails on their jeans. Slack was a short, quiet fellow who didn't leave distinct impressions; when a question arose, he let Arnold handle it. Arnold was a long, articulate stringbean with a face full of honest excitement. He was known to have served with Morgan's Raiders during the Civil War and, regardless of sentiments, a guerilla-fighter was a straight shooter.

The picturesque pair didn't ride into town shouting their discovery up Market Street, of course. They arrived on a Union Pacific train on the first or second day of the month, Arnold carrying a canvas sack and Slack beside him dangling a Winchester in the crook of his right arm. After checking into a hotel they went out for a drink, carrying the sack and standing it upright on the floor between them as they bent their elbows. Wherever they went, the sack went with them.

By the middle of February half the barkeeps in San

Francisco were conjecturing on the contents of the bag and wondering why it received such close attention. Their interest was also piqued when the sourdoughs conducted all conversation in a whisper. One tavern owner said they seemed frightened, as if they had something too hot to handle, too good to let go.

Either way, the sack was at least heavy, and so Arnold and Slack carried it into the Bank of California and asked to have it deposited in a vault. No sooner had they received a receipt and departed than the inquisitive cashier was in a back room inspecting the contents. He found precious stones—a bagful of rough, uncut diamonds, emeralds, sapphires, and rubies. That was too hot for *him* to handle, so he took his discovery to the bank's president, William C. Ralston.

Bill Ralston was one of San Francisco's big men. He was an investment banker with a free wheeling urge to take a chance. Rarely losing on a venture, he had put together a fortune that elevated him to ranking position among the city's elite. When he peered into the canvas, rubbed the gems in his hands, and heard about the whiskered men, he decided that a big deal was lurking. But being a sharply honed man for all his flamboyancy, he called in an assayer to inspect the stones on a confidential basis. The expert said they were worth about $125,000 and must have been taken out of the ground fairly recently.

Ralston decided that the approach to Arnold, the Civil War veteran, should be made through channels of military camaraderie. So he confided his discovery to an occasional investment partner, George D. Roberts, who had come out of the war as a Union Army general. Roberts immediately suspected that Arnold was the man who had investigated some mining properties for him only two years earlier. At their first meeting the general was delighted; it was the same Arnold.

Roberts seated the sourdoughs around several bottles of good liquor and soon he and Arnold were reliving adventures from Sumter to Appomattox. Although they had fought on opposite sides, new friendships were stronger than old animosities, they agreed.

And so they got down, eventually, to the amazing gem discovery, which caused Arnold to fall back into whispers.

"I thought it would blind us," he said. "We came onto the field and the glittering in the sun was so strong we blinked. Everywhere we turned we saw the stones. Slack here went wild. He dug away with a boot heel and scratched them right out of the ground."

The general's eyes stared glassily. He could almost see the gem field himself. "You fellows are in for a fortune," he said, "if you can just get those stones out of there." He poured another drink and let them ponder his remark.

Arnold and Slack stared uneasily at each other. Then Arnold unburdened himself. "General," he said, "that's what has us stirred up. We've got hold of this thing but we don't know what to do with it. If we start hauling the stones out in sacks, someone'll trace the field. The only way to do it is to tie up the land and bring rigs in to mine it out. But we can't get money for that without selling what we brought out and that would raise suspicion. Now, we don't know who's got that kind of money and some kind of honesty."

The general nodded sympathetically. It was a dilemma he could understand. He talked for fifteen minutes about the sad state of mankind's morals, how things had come to where one human being couldn't trust another. Then he brightened.

"Tell you men what I'll do," he said. "I don't have that kind of money myself, but I'm close to men who do. I can take the problem to them and see if they won't agree to finance a company that would obtain legal title to the field and mine the stones. Naturally, you would be partners in the company. Now, how does that sound?"

Slack seemed just a bit suspicious of the general, but it was clear that Arnold was running the show. He agreed and Slack subsided. But that was as far as the general got. Try as he would, he could not get the pair to tell him where they had made their great discovery.

By the following morning several pressures were working through San Francisco. The cashier who had received the sourdoughs' sack began using his discovery as a conversation piece and Arnold and Slack found themselves a magnet for the curious and acquisitive. They stopped denying their find, but refused to discuss its location, even vaguely. One evening, however, Arnold seemed to have a drink too many and hinted that the field was west of Omaha and south of Laramie. Despite the fact that this narrowed the field to but half the West, a rumor whistled through town that the cornucopia was in the northeast corner of Arizona, where part of the Navajo Indian reservation is located today. Within a week, fully a thousand men had departed in search of remarkable riches.

Another pressure came from banker Bill Ralston. General Roberts, feeling that he had cut himself in by laying the groundwork, handed the problem of Arnold's and Slack's silence back to Ralston, who had the most persuasive tongue south of the Columbia River. Soon the banker was showing the sourdoughs, in terms they could almost feel, what exploitation of the gem field would mean to them. He spoke of mansions, wine cellars, servants, carriages, women, and position in the community of the rich.

Arnold's hands trembled by the minute as Ralston orated. When he could no longer contain himself he burst out with, "You've got a deal, Mr. Ralston."

"Call me Bill, boys," Ralston said.

Bill got the excited pair to agree to lead two of his associates into the field for a thorough inspection. Arnold insisted on only one caution: Ralston's representatives must be blindfolded until they reached the field.

Two weeks later, when the party returned to San Francisco, the banker's associates were dazed. They didn't know where they'd been, but they had seen more jewels than they could count, and had brought back a bag of them. "Not because we thought anyone would doubt us," they told Ralston, "but because we wanted to be sure ourselves that we hadn't been dreaming."

With Ralston's acquiescence, the news leaked out. It spread through the city as fast as the fire of thirty-odd years later. People accepted the reports without doubt, for the gem find was simply another proof of what they fervently believed: the West, and San Francisco in particular, was fated to become the richest, most powerful area in the burgeoning United States. Without using the exact phrase, civic leaders talked of the city's manifest destiny.

They had ample evidence. The West was still riding a crest of enthusiasm that followed the purchase of Alaska five years earlier. True, some were calling the purchase

Seward's Folly, but Westerners knew you couldn't go far wrong for two cents an acre, especially when those acres might contain fabulous fur and mineral riches. And only recently they had enjoyed the golden spike ceremony, the joining of the Central and Union Pacific Railroads that made San Francisco easily accessible to the rest of the growing nation.

As Easterners traveled west for the first time, they found an area that almost constituted a separate nation, a vastness and beauty they had not realized was part of their birthright. Foreigners were awed, too. In 1869 an Englishman had visited Utah and Colorado and returned home to announce that he had discovered several mountains of pure silver. When he offered to share his mountains with people who would invest three million dollars to make molehills out of them, the *Times of London* exposed him as a fraud and he disappeared, but the debacle dampened no enthusiasm for the American West.

That was the prevailing spirit of confidence which led San Franciscans to place wholehearted faith in Arnold's and Slack's Western gem field. Twenty-five bold citizens gave banker Ralston $80,000 apiece to get in on the ground floor of the new San Francisco and New York Mining and Commercial Company. Then Baron Ferdinand Rothschild of London and Paris came in and so did a couple of New Yorkers named Horace Greeley and Charles Tiffany. Greeley had left the New York *Tribune* but was still a formidable name, and Tiffany was the founder of the noted Fifth Avenue jewelry firm.

With over $2,000,000 in capital at his disposal, Bill Ralston continued to combine caution with a keen sense of public relations. He told Arnold and Slack he wanted to submit their bag of gems to Tiffany, the most noted American authority on precious stones. The sourdoughs quickly agreed, which set the scene for a publicity-laden meeting at Tiffany's offices in New York. Present, in addition to the luminaries mentioned, was Abe Lincoln's unsuccessful presidential opponent, General George B. McClellan, one of the directors of the firm.

When everyone was seated and the reporters had been briefed, Ralston approached a large table at which Tiffany sat. He carried a sack of stones which, with some effort, he lifted and upended. The gems spilled into a large heap before Tiffany, and the audience gasped. The jeweler fingered a few and rubbed them. He held them up to the light and finally subjected them to searching inspection through a jeweler's glass.

"These are precious stones of enormous value," he said.

"How much value?" Bill Ralston asked.

"I will have to submit them to my lapidaries for an exact appraisal," Tiffany replied. The fact was that the jeweler knew next to nothing about uncut diamonds.

For forty-eight hours the newspapers kept the story boiling, and then came the verdict. When cut, the gems would be worth $150,000. Ralston, who had brought only a tenth of the stones from his vaults, hurried down to Washington to conduct some further business. He looked up Senator Ben Butler and hired him as a legal consultant. Butler, a Westerner whom the Senate looked to in matters of mining and minerals, agreed that he would be invaluable in getting Congress to legalize the firm's claim to the gem field.

It might seem that Bill Ralston had subjected the sourdoughs' veracity to the ultimate test. But no. An insatiable pursuer of peace of mind, he suggested that, as a last condition the field be examined by a consulting engineer whose reputation was without a blemish. When Arnold and Slack again agreed, Ralston retained Henry Janin, an engineer so conservative in appraisals that he was said to have approved five hundred mines in which clients later prospered, none in which they lost money. Janin received his price: $2,500, all his expenses, and the right to buy shares in the firm at a low price.

Again Arnold and Slack interruped the gracious life they were enjoying in San Francisco, on a cash advance of $100,000 made by Ralston, and conducted a blindfolded expedition to their Shangri-la. But this time Arnold laid the groundwork for his exit by first protesting bitterly that he and Slack were being put to immense trouble. When they returned to San Francisco this time, Janin added his expert opinion to the others that had confirmed the find. Soon Ralston was turning down offers of as much as $200,000, plus twenty percent royalties, for one-acre claims near the still undisclosed site. One hundred thousand shares of stock in the mining company were issued and distributed among the original investors; this was too good a thing to let the grubby public share.

But Ralston found that Arnold's patience had been too sorely tried, and Slack's emotions slavishly followed suit. Arnold said that while the big-money men had set themselves up to earn a fortune, he and Slack had been continually stalled. He wanted out, and would settle for $550,000. Ralston happily paid it in cash and said a fond farewell to the sourdoughs, who divulged the location of the gem field and immediately left town—Slack to disappear forever and Arnold to return to his birthplace in northern Kentucky, where he was triumphantly received as a true and successful son of the South.

Knowing nothing of these startling developments, Clarence King, a young geologist, arrived in San Francisco in September, 1872, after having spent the better part of five years studying the mineral lands of the West. King was a product of Yale, and, at thirty, a scientist respected for both theoretical and practical knowledge. One of his most recent tasks had been to survey the Fortieth Parallel for the government, which was why he received the gem field news with considerable surprise. He had reported that the geological makeup of Nevada, Utah, Colorado, and Wyoming showed no possibility of precious stone formations. He doubted that Arizona would be an exception.

King found Janin, whom he knew, and got the entire story. The engineer, still high with excitement, said he and Arnold had traveled thirty-six hours on the Union Pacific before debarking in western Wyoming.

"Then he blindfolded me," Janin related, "and put me on a horse. We rode for two days with the sun in our faces a lot of the time. When we got there and Arnold took my blindfold off, I saw the most beautiful view I've ever come across. We were high, I figure about 7,000 feet, and standing on a mesa that was mostly desert, but right near us was a conical mountain with a flat top. That was the field. In ten minutes I dug out maybe $10,000 worth of stones. They were everywhere, in gulches, between rocks and in shallow holes. Clarence, you ought to get in on this yourself. I know you said there wouldn't be diamonds around the Fortieth Parallel, but swallow your pride and take a look yourself. Anybody can make a mistake, Clarence."

King would swallow neither his pride nor Janin's story. Instead, he reviewed the method by which the engineer had been taken to the gem field. Arizona was out of the question, he decided, because two day's ride from Wyoming would only get a man halfway. Then he recalled that Janin had said the sun was in his face "a lot of the time." To the suspicious King, that sounded as if the engineer had been sandbagged. He had been led back and forth over the same general area for a couple of days. So King went back over his Rocky Mountain field notes and found a description that matched Janin's. He was not precise in his recollection of the mountain, but he knew it was somewhere in eastern Utah, in the Uinta Mountain foothills, just south of the Wyoming line.

Taking the Central Pacific line into Wyoming, he located an old prospector who had cared for his pack horses during geological expeditions. Together they scoured the Uinta foothills country until they reached a lofty elevation. There they found the conical mountain. It was no more than twenty-five miles south of the Central Pacific tracks. King grinned as he recalled that when Janin told Arnold he thought he heard a train whistle, the Kentuckian said, "You're suffering from gem fever, man! That was an Indian yell."

While King bedded down for the night, his helper, intrigued by the story of the gems, began scratching in the sandy soil. Ten minutes later he brought King a large, rough diamond. He had found it in a hole that, on inspection, looked as if it had been made by a miner's steel tool. Then, as King was dropping off to sleep, the old prospector whooped.

"Mr. King," he shouted, "this is the greatest gem field in the world. It even produces cut diamonds!"

Sure enough, he held a stone whose face had felt the knife of a lapidary.

In the morning King went to work. He found sapphires, rubies, garnets, and emeralds, a disparate collection that nature could not possibly produce in one area. He found them stuck between rocks that showed tool marks under a magnifying glass; rocks without scratches yielded no stones. He even found a diamond in the crook of a tree branch. The field ran over a quarter-mile area and ended as abruptly as it started. It had obviously been salted, loaded with stones that nature had manufactured in various parts of the world, but never in the American West.

King and the prospector rode out to the railroad station, where the geologist wired Ralston that he had been duped. The banker refused to believe it until he established King's identity. Then he wired back that he and Janin were coming out to Wyoming and wanted King to lead them into the land of the deflated bauble. King obliged, and the end of the saga came quickly.

The San Francisco and New York Mining and Commercial Company retreated into obscurity and embarrassed explanations were issued to a bewildered public: Ralston and General Roberts had been taken in by greed fed on rumor; Tiffany was totally unfamiliar with raw diamonds, as were his lapidaries, and had been psychologically prepared to feel that the stones were genuine; Janin, having been called in only after eminent figures had endorsed the field, was also ready to believe anything.

The deluded San Franciscans finally pieced together the story of how they had been fleeced. Arnold and Slack had gone to Europe in 1871 and visited several Amsterdam diamond merchants. All they ever showed interest in were low-grade diamonds, stones that had been rejected because of flaws or poor coloration. The merchants called the pair "the dumb Americans." Then they suddenly departed for London, where they stimulated additional disrespect for American intelligence. Altogether, they spent almost $50,000 for the biggest mess of low quality, rough diamonds ever collected by anybody. As a bonus of inadvertence, they also got the polished diamond which Clarence King's helper came onto after they had returned to America and salted the Uinta foothill.

Banker Ralston knew that since Kentucky was still not gently disposed toward Northerners and particularly Northerners who called a Southerner a swindler, he would never get $650,000 worth of satisfaction out of Arnold on his home ground.

But one investor, whose bitterness was proportionate to the amount of greed that had led him to buy out other investors, traveled down to Kentucky and found Arnold in Elizabethtown, operating as a highly respected banker. He initiated such a pester of legal actions that Arnold finally bought immunity from prosecution by returning $150,000. The rest he used to finance his bank's expansion, an action that so vexed the other bank in town that its owner strolled up to Arnold one day and shot him dead.

The West was still without native-born diamonds, but it was not lacking in excitement. Two years after the exposure of the great diamond fraud, Bill Ralston's Bank of California failed under the weight of his wild speculations. Ralston, short by $5,000,000, was found floating in San Francisco Bay. The ghost who stalks abandoned old mines —even non-existent gem fields—had claimed its final victim.

CHAPTER IX

The Man Who Gave Henry Ford a Ride

LOUIS ENRICHT was a man who never promised the ordinary. He specialized in pledging the miraculous, and in presenting each miracle as more stupendous than the previous. His career was unusual in that he swindled boldly from 1890 on, but remained obscure until 1916, when he was seventy years old. It was then that he offered the world his most fabulous discovery.

He said he had found a substitute for gasoline that could be manufactured for a penny a gallon.

Since gasoline was selling at thirty times that price and was scarce because of the war raging in Europe, Enricht became a sensation overnight. He found himself a subject of controversy between warring governments, an object of investment to Henry Ford, and an inspiration to crackpots the world over.

But after Enricht had become considerably wealthier as a result, he was—like many swindlers—only a source of extreme embarrassment to those who had coveted him and his "secret."

On the afternoon of April 11, 1916, Enricht faced a score of skeptical reporters who stood and sat on his small, trim lawn in rustic Farmingdale, Long Island. Some of the newsmen exchanged quips about the old man's bushy gray mustache, which flowed from above his lip down past his mouth, as they waited for what they expected would develop into a humorous feature about a harmless crank.

Then Enricht silenced them with his announcement.

"I have learned to do what chemists have been dreaming of for years," he said. "I can transform water into gasoline by the addition of a chemical that has been compounded under a secret formula!"

The reporters chuckled in disbelief, but the towering, white-haired man glowered down on them and said he would demonstrate the power of his discovery. From a garage behind his modest, white-frame house appeared Louis Enricht, Jr., who at twenty-six was emulating his father's glorious mustache with only weedy success. Junior handed Enricht a small vial and the old man turned to an automobile in his driveway.

He thrust a long stick into its gas tank and pulled it out dry. He tapped the tank and it rang hollow. The reporters pressed forward and peered through the tank's filler opening to convince themselves it had no false bottom or sides.

Enricht picked up a white china pitcher, filled it from a garden hose, and offered it to a reporter, who tasted it and said, "Pure water, nothing else." Then the son held the pitcher while the father poured in a green-tinted fluid. Enricht stirred the mixture and dumped it into the gasoline tank. Junior cranked and the engine caught and raced fiercely.

The reporters buzzed among themselves, no longer laughing. Enricht watched cheerfully as two of them climbed into the car and drove it around the village of Farmingdale. They returned enthusiastic, whereupon the old man kissed his petite, silver-haired wife, Anna, who had come out to watch, and strolled back into his home.

The reporters rushed off to tell the world how they had witnessed a penny-a-gallon chemical operate an automobile with water.

Enricht realized that his sensational announcement would inevitably be greeted with some skepticism, and that his first task would be to deal with the skeptics—one of whom appeared almost immediately. He was William E. Haskell, publisher of the Chicago *Herald*. Haskell had bought his first motor car back in 1895, and felt he was an automotive authority. He arrived in Farmingdale, eager but reserved, on the Sunday after Enricht's first demonstration. "I am frank to confess," he said, "that I approach the proposition with caution."

Haskell found Enricht no less cautious—or rather, just as prepared. "So many Standard Oil agents have been here disguised as newspapermen," the self-styled inventor said, "that I must be careful to know who I'm dealing with." He explained that Standard Oil was his enemy because the firm had snubbed him twenty-five years earlier when he had offered it a secret that would have saved it thousands of dollars a year. He had asked for $20,000, but Standard had tried to get his secret for $1,500. That was all but banditry, he said, and he hadn't sold.

Haskell was more than a little impressed, but he grew

suspicious again when he touched a drop of Enricht's green fluid to his lips. He smacked and asked darkly, "What's that bitter almond odor?"

"Prussic acid," Enricht replied. "I put it in to disguise another odor that would come up strong and identify the formula's more important ingredients."

The inventor explained morosely that his discovery had brought him a dilemma. He would probably have to sell for a song because chemical analysis of the formula's ingredients would be easy. The ingredients, he said, were "so cheap and common that no one could possibly corner the market on them. This means that anyone can manufacture the substitute. It's the secret that is complex—not the manufacture after the parts are known. This green fluid is a white elephant."

Enricht's long, lined face was bleak as he demonstrated the formula for Haskell, who had first satisfied himself that the car had no hidden fuel supply and that its gas tank had no false bottom.

"A couple of turns at the crank and the engine started, racing fiercely with an open throttle," Haskell reported. "It ran even and true. I got in the car and drove it all around Farmingdale, and never had a bit of trouble. It was a most remarkable demonstration indeed."

That evening the publisher departed for Chicago to write that he had just sat in on "the beginning of an industrial revolution."

"If anyone had tried to convince me of what I witnessed myself," he added, "I could not have believed him."

The gasoline substitute was big news, as Enricht had correctly figured it would be. The soaring price of motor fuel was approaching thirty cents a gallon; at the very

moment Enricht was demonstrating for Haskell, thousands
of Pittsburghers, led by a police motorcycle escort, were
parading demands for a Federal investigation. And there
was the World War. England was fighting Germany,
America's sympathies were obvious, and essential gasoline
supplies were low. Chemical engineers were spending a
good deal of their time lecturing on the urgent need to
find a cheap and plentiful substitute.

And that, said Louis Enricht, a man who understood the
art of timing, was exactly what he had found. One pound
of his green magic mixed with water, he said, would produce 667 pounds of fuel. His telephone rang incessantly
and every day mailmen delivered two hundred offers of
financial assistance in puttting the remarkable discovery
on the market. Enricht, biding his time, put all the letters
into a carton, and stored the carton in his attic.

Two days after the demonstration for Publisher Haskell,
the reporters returned, hungry for more news, and Enricht
did not send them away unsatisfied. He cannily let slip
what he called a "principal secret of my formula." He said
his chemical was not combustible in itself, but that it had
a passionate affinity for the oxygen in water. This affinity
caused the oxygen to separate from the hydrogen. When
the hydrogen atoms were released, they combined in a
violent manner with the next nearest oxygen atoms, those
in the air. This resounding, shotgun-type marriage produced an explosion, which created the power. It was as
simple and as enchanting as that.

But, worse luck, not everyone was enchanted. Dr.
Thomas B. Freas, associate professor of chemistry at Columbia University, took sharp and public exception. "No
chemical can be added to water that will make it com-

bustible," he declared. "Water may be broken up by electrolysis, but the energy required will be exactly equal to that produced on burning. That is, nothing would be gained. Absolutely nothing."

Sniffing a controversy, newsmen dashed this heresy out to Farmingdale. "The professor says your idea is impractical," one of them told Enricht.

His nimble mind was more than equal to such skepticism. "That's nothing," he replied easily. "They always say that when an important discovery is made."

But then an even more forceful dissent was heard. Dr. C. F. Chandler, a founder of the Columbia University School of Mines and a scientist of international standing, said: "The proposition is absolutely impossible. It's trying to get something out of nothing." Dr. Chandler said several substances—metallic sodium, for one—would release hydrogen from water most effectively. "But to get enough hydrogen to equal the energy in one gallon of gasoline would take fifty-seven and a half pounds of sodium," he added. "At twenty-five cents a pound, such energy would cost $14.37."

Enricht laughed grimly. "It's fortunate I'm not using metallic sodium, isn't it?" he stated.

With public curiosity at the spillway, Ferdinand Jehle, laboratory engineer of the Automobile Club of America, then asked Enricht to submit a sample to test, pledging that no attempt would be made to discover the formula's constituents. "We want to find out if it's of value," Jehle said, "or to be plain, if it's fake."

"Call it a fake if you like," Enricht retorted. "It makes no difference to me." But while he was talking, he was thinking, and the result was a decision to call up a diversion. He invited the reporters to talk to a gentleman whose word could not be questioned. That gentleman was Benjamin Franklin Yoakum, a financier, board member of several railways and one-time president of the St. Louis and San Francisco Railroad. Yoakum lived on Fifth Avenue in New York and was a member of the proper clubs, but he was also a summer neighbor of Enricht's, owning a large estate just outside Farmingdale. All this made him a scientific authority, too, naturally.

"I have known Louis Enricht a long time," Yoakum said. "I have confidence in his invention. I have used it in my own motor car." He added that his interest in Enricht was not financial; he simply wanted to see cheaper motive power developed.

The skeptics held their fire and a clamor arose for a public demonstration. Everyone wanted to see the green liquid marvel. Enricht, feeling the need for another diversion, refused to give any further demonstrations, but his refusal earned only sympathy.

"I could not demonstrate it if I wanted to," he said, "for I am about out of material. I went into New York to buy some, but found it would not be safe. I was being followed. At a restaurant, a man watched from out in the street. And when I went to a chemist, he came there, too." Enricht said he had bought five tubes of petroleum jelly and returned home.

Into this shadowy atmosphere now slipped a strange man who had made industrial history once and longed to do it again. He was Henry Ford, whose publicity man flew up from Washington and drove out to Farmingdale. The press agent, Theodore Delavigne, handed Enricht a telegram he had received from Ford: "Put Mr. Enricht aboard the Wolverine Express and, rain or shine, deliver him f.o.b. at my office in Detroit."

Enricht was courteous, but declined the rail ticket. He said he was afraid to carry his secret formula with him and afraid to leave it home, even though he had reduced it to code.

The following Monday, just thirteen days after the first revelation of the discovery, the New York *Times* headlined the extent of Ford's interest:

FORD SEES ENRICHT
ABOUT MOTOR FUEL

———

Inventor Talks for an Hour, and
Ford Will Come Again and See
Cent-a-Gallon Mixture Work

How could Henry Ford get involved with Louis Enricht? How, for that matter, could he not? The fifty-two-year-old tycoon was as ornery and unpredictable as he was gifted. It was utterly in character that this remarkable inventor should hurry to Long Island himself to see and touch and hear Enricht. After a meeting in the Brown Hotel in Farmingdale, Gaston Plantiff, Ford's New York sales manager, announced: "He thought it was worth following up; that is about all that can be said." That is all that should have been said, but Plantiff could not resist going on. "Mr. Ford is careful in his moves, going forward a step at a time," he said, unconscious of the fact that everything in Ford's life belied such a remark. "You see, Mr. Ford is something of a chemist himself and he no doubt could ask Mr. Enricht a number of questions. The answers must not have been unsatisfactory or the matter would have been dropped."

It wasn't. The next day the motor magnate declared he would buy Enricht's formula outright if it passed tests. "I wrote Mr. Enricht today," Ford said. "We will have a test in a week or so and I'll be there. I don't know what to think of it but we've had men working along that line for some time."

Enricht himself would say nothing of his relations with Ford. He smiled coyly and hummed a pleasant little tune as he, his wife Anna, and Louis, Jr. went for neighborhood walks. The world, its appetite stimulated by the newspapers, hungered for more miracles.

Not that people were without news of other remarkable events in this field. One of the fascinating features of Enricht's initial announcement is that, in the period that followed, an astonishing number of similar gasoline-from-practically-nothing schemes received wide publicity. A Detroit laboratory was producing a fuel that had been "reatomized" so none could reach auto engine cylinders in liquid form; a saving of fifty percent was promised. A Trenton, New Jersey, inventor demonstrated "gasafoam," which was produced by agitating various oils and would sell for ten cents a gallon. A Newark grain dealer announced he had invented "gasene," a mixture of gasoline, kerosene, and an inexpensive chemical; he was selling it at seven cents a gallon below the price of gasoline.

From South Africa came word of "Natalite," made of ether and alcohol. "Natalite" delivered twenty-six miles to the gallon, it was said. And a Danish chemist said he had invented "Nuoline," a ten-cent-a-gallon potion of water, naphthaline, camphor, and an extract of hard coal.

But Canadian Forest Rangers topped the Dane. They were making a new motor fuel from sawdust and wood chips— by a secret method, of course.

And finally the climax. Harrison G. Shoupe, a pioneer auto man, announced in Sandusky, Ohio that he had discovered a way of making gasoline out of water, à la Enricht. A wealthy Chicagoan promptly agreed to pay him $10,000 plus $500 a month for life, and arrived with a chemist to begin exploiting the process. When Shoupe could not produce water-gasoline by his process, the chemist investigated and found two hidden pipes, one connected to a can of standard gasoline.

All this was like contagion, but it was also quite in the pattern. When a swindler comes up with a "revolutionary scientific discovery," several others—swindlers and merely crackpots—immediately claim the bounder had stolen their life's work. The psychopathic personality needs little stimulation to begin weaving fantasies.

This, of course, implies that some considered Enricht a swindler. Very few felt that way—that is, until April 27, 1916, less than a month after his opening performance. It was then that folksy Farmingdale picked up its morning newspapers and read that their suddenly famous neighbor was more than an aged refugee from the severe winters of the Midwest.

Enricht, it was revealed, was a German who had emigrated to this country in his early twenties. He had no particular skills but he did have a stern manner that bespoke honesty and straightforwardness. He had not had even a smattering of scientific training and worked mostly as a salesman. All through the years in the New World, he longed to have wife Anna look up to him as a man of accomplishment, and at the age of forty-four, he succeeded. Deciding that a railroad line from Canyon City, Colorado, to Cripple Creek was desperately needed, he collected funds to build it. That was in 1890. When, in 1903, no track had yet been laid, bankruptcy separated the investors from their investments and Enricht was arrested. But no one could make a charge stick, and he was released.

Seven years later, in Chicago, he gave Anna and his son more to admire when he began selling 45,000 acres of the vast Cumberland Plateau in Kentucky and Tennessee. He operated with what he described as deeds handed down in Colonial days by Patrick Henry. Enricht was indicted for using the mails to defraud, fined $500, and warned to be careful how he used U. S. postage in the future. Anna didn't understand such matters; she knew, though, that something important was always going on around her husband.

The presumably chastened fellow went to New York and dabbled in the stock market, but in 1912 he again entered bankruptcy. Looking around for another outlet for his boundless imagination and energy, he somehow interested a number of wealthy Englishmen in a formula for making artificial stone. This time, he meticulously kept his transactions out of the mails. The Englishmen gave him a considerable amount of money when he claimed he could make stone out of sand, ashes, or sawdust, that he could turn a swamp into a concrete bridge in six hours, and that he had a railroad tie transformed from sawdust. But when he delivered the formula, the Englishmen strongly intimated that they had been fleeced. Enricht was so hurt he quietly left the city and settled in Farmingdale.

Those were the revelations the newspapers printed, and they made it unmistakably clear that the quiet villager was, in reality, an inexhaustible ragbag of swindlery.

But was that really clear? Not, apparently, to Henry Ford, for as dusk of that day fell on Long Island, the Model T genius reappeared. Ford drove up and closeted himself with the charlatan in a garage. At midnight, after Enricht had asked for forgiveness for the big-boned skeletons in his past, Ford departed with a promise to send a new car for experimental use. He did, and added another expression of his cavernous inability to accept the obvious—$1,000 in cash.

The townsfolk of Farmingdale should have been slower than Ford to forgive, for many of them, it emerged, had been patronizing a curious Enricht sideline. Their neighbor had been selling them bottles of "radium water" and a tonic that was supposed to make their hens more prolific egg layers. Now the villagers began reassessing the virtues of these nonsensical products, but they were diverted by an electrifying series of events.

This time the old man's salvation came from the huge Maxim Munitions Corporation of New Jersey, manufacturers of ammunition and bayonets. Ignoring the wrinkles and dents in Enricht's character, the firm announced it had arranged for exclusive rights to manufacture his gasoline substitute. Maxim said it would buy land in Farmingdale on which to build a laboratory and factory. It applied for a patent and cheerfully promised that motorists would not be the only ones to benefit; farmers would get cheap power for wood sawing and threshing. "Experiments prove that Enricht's invention, perfected in some minor details, will be revolutionary in character," the company said.

If anyone thought Maxim's action seemed incredible in light of the exposure of the old man's past, he would have been overwhelmed by reports of the high finances involved. "It was said that Enricht received one million in cash and 100,000 shares of Maxim stock" ($10.50 a share), said *Patent News*, the inventor's journal. *Patent News* called him "Dr." Enricht. With so much money involved, how could the "doctor" be thought dishonest?

Henry Ford, shocked at Enricht's duplicity, opened a futile campaign to retain rights to the invention. Ford's agent was asked if the Ford Company would discontinue its tests. "No," he said, "we are going ahead as before. I was talking with Mr. Enricht today and he said there was absolutely no truth in the statement that Maxim Munitions had acquired the rights to the mixture."

The next round went to Maxim, whose treasurer said, "I do not think Mr. Enricht was correctly understood. We certainly have the contract."

Thus, men who were considered wise old business heads endowed Enricht with a new mantle of respectability. The New York *Times*, which had supplied its share of scoffing, commented in an editorial:

It looks at least a little as if the wise ones had been somewhat hasty in saying offhand what can and can't be done, and it may be that—not for the first time—they are to be proven wrong by an inventor whose pretensions they had loftily ridiculed.

Henry Ford, now furious, sued to recover his automobile. Then, probably on strong advice, he suddenly dropped from the scene to run (unsuccessfully) for the

United States Senate and dream of becoming president. So ownership of Enricht's formula seemed settled—except that nothing remained settled for long in this bizarre story.

Maxim Munitions, in the kind of action that drives newspapermen to drink, pulled in its horns after the price of its stock had doubled and denied it had made any deal with Enricht. Hudson Maxim, the firm's consulting engineer, said in a letter to the *Times*, "Why, I haven't even met Enricht."

Although the statement sounded definite enough, it was heavily discounted in light of the signs of wealth that suddenly sprouted all over Enricht's Farmingdale property. There the old man had begun work on a laboratory and ordered architect's plans for a new home. He said he would build a large factory of his own, too.

An artist at making diversion as mighty as the sword, he also decided to reveal that he had found a substitute for Babbitt metal, the antimony-tin-copper-lead alloy used in motor bearings. His alloy, he said, would have an even stronger anti-friction quality than that which Isaac Babbitt had devised, and it would be seventy-five percent cheaper. As reporters scribbled furiously, Enricht dropped in the additional revelation that he was experimenting with a revolutionary new method of extracting nitrogen from the air for use in explosives and fertilizers. The old man was never at a loss for inventions.

Now, however, no one laughed out loud. Those who took exception to his free wheeling mental processes kept their own counsel. But since there were few developments to keep the Enricht story humming, he gradually slipped out of the newspaper columns. The supposition was that he was perfecting his gasoline discovery. Then the United

States entered World War I and eight months later, the day after Thanksgiving, 1917, his name bounced back onto the front pages.

Railroad financier Benjamin Yoakum made the big news this time. He revealed that the Maxim firm's little heeded disclaimer *had* been true. Maxim had not acquired rights to Enricht's formula. The man who had supplied the inventor with his new wealth was Yoakum himself. He had closed a deal on April 12, 1917, six days after the U. S. had entered the war. He and Enricht now controlled a firm known as the National Motor Power Company, which was to produce auto fuel from the Enricht formula.

But that was only a prelude to a shocking charge that Yoakum made public. In Nassau County Supreme Court, he contended that Enricht was refusing to make his formula available to our government. Furthermore, Yoakum charged, Enricht had dickered with "spies and representatives of the German government" to sell the formula for a million and a half dollars. Thus was joined a second great battle of futility.

The difficulties began, Yoakum explained, when a British Army technical officer made exhaustive tests of Enricht's method, went back to England with a favorable report, and returned with authority to buy.

"When the company called on Enricht to go ahead with the work," Yoakum declared, "he confessed he had withheld an essential ingredient from the formula he had given us. He handed us a signed statement in which he asserted he would not go on with the project during the war. So we started an investigation."

Yoakum had put private detectives on Enricht's trail. They reported that he had met secretly with Captain

Franz von Papen, who had been the military attaché of the German Embassy in Washington until he was expelled by the U. S. State Department (and went on to become one of Hitler's aides). Enricht's meeting took place, the detectives said, while the submarine *Deutschland* was tied up in Baltimore Harbor from July 1 to August 3, 1916.

Naturally, Yoakum was upset. "We have grave fears," he said, "that Enricht has already disclosed his secret to the German government, and that the seeming plentifulness of gasoline in that country is due to the fact that they are manufacturing Enricht's liquid on a large scale." Accordingly, Yoakum asked U. S. Attorney General Thomas W. Gregory to seize the inventor's papers and plant. Gregory could not act without proof, so now Yoakum wanted the courts to intervene.

Which they did. An injunction restrained Enricht from disposing of his formula and the Nassau County sheriff threw guards around the Farmingdale laboratory. Enricht, who could have been expected to grow nervous under the gravity of such charges, showed instead that he had the situation more in hand than his adversaries. "Absurd," he said quietly, and then offered one of his complex, many tributaried explanations. He conceded he had met Von Papen, but said they had discussed his "new system of making artificial stone." Von Papen, he said, offered him $10,000. "I laughed at him." To close the matter, Enricht inserted a couple of typical confusions: "I am a patriot. If the government wants my process for extracting nitrogen from the air, it can have it." He also revealed that inflation had increased his costs, and that his penny-a-gallon substitute might have to be sold for as much as four cents.

Yoakum, trying desperately to be heard above this comic-opera noise, stuck with the matter at hand and won a court order to search Enricht's safe deposit box in the First National Bank of Farmingdale. Nothing was found but twenty Liberty bonds. Enricht said he had burned the formula.

Yoakum was defeated. No one had ever held the highly publicized formula but Enricht, which meant no case could be made; there was only hearsay evidence. The railroader took his loss, described by the administrator of his estate as substantial, and went on to invest in a scheme to extract more gasoline from crude oil with a special furnace. Like Enricht, the furnace burned him financially.

As for the United States government, which was presumably deprived of a secret weapon, it chose to let the affair fade away and to muddle through the war without Enricht's formula.

That might have been the end of the green-magic gasoline swindle, but it was by no means the end of swindler Louis Enricht's capers. With monumental casualness he retreated into a $20,000 home which, in those days, was a good bit of home, and planned new enterprises.

Now seventy-two years old, Enricht proved he was incorrigible. He closed 1920 by seeking a patent on yet another wondrous invention—a process for making gasoline of peat. "I can get 460 gallons out of one ton of common peat," he asserted. Patent Office technicians turned him down on grounds his scheme was contrary to all known laws of chemistry, but such timidity failed to discourage the indomitable fellow. He went right on making gasoline out of peat, or in any event saying he was, through a stock firm known as the Enricht Peat

Gasoline Corporation. Fresh investors, believe it or not, rushed in where chemists feared to tread, and brought over $40,000 with them. Enricht proceeded to build what he called a gasoline manufacturing plant, five miles south of Farmingdale.

This venture inevitably led to the creaky old man's indictment a year later for grand larceny. Specifically, he was charged with using investors' checks for personal purposes, but that did not keep him from bailing himself out with a $2,000 check made out to the firm. He explained that he would give the company some stock in return. In October, 1922, when he came to trial in Nassau County's rambling, high-domed Old Courthouse, Justice Lewis J. Smith became entranced with the scientific aspects of the case and asked him if he could really make gasoline out of peat.

"Certainly," the unquenchable one replied. "I will demonstrate the machine in court."

The following afternoon he arrived with a machine and a load of peat. A fascinated crowd gawked as he worked from two to five o'clock in the afternoon setting up the contraption. When it was assembled, he dropped several handfuls of peat in, added a few pails of water, ignited a blowtorch and waved it at a bailiff, then lit the peat. Court attendants worked a suction pump and a compressor until they were exhausted, but no gasoline flowed. Enricht explained that the compressor was leaking and said he would renew his demonstration the next afternoon.

Justice Smith, patient but only human, said no. Then a Patent Office official threw cold water on the peat theory, and another witness testified that the only gasoline

Enricht's machine produced came from an underground tank and a hose. The jury found him guilty of larceny.

Justice Smith, who could have imposed a lengthy sentence, gave the doddering old fellow five to nine years unless he repaid the investors. Enricht said he would, by selling his 20,000 Georgia acres. Four months later he was back, having failed to repay a cent. On February 28, 1923, Justice Smith re-sentenced him to three to seven years and committed him to Sing Sing the same day.

Today, the Nassau County Court's chief clerk, who was twenty-one at the time, recalls Enricht as a pathetic frame of a man standing for the last time before the bench. His trademark mustache had grown so long it was part of his beard. His eyes were cloudy and he seemed not to comprehend all that was taking place.

A year and eighteen days later, Governor Alfred E. Smith was moved to commute Enricht's sentence to time served. In April, 1924, at the age of seventy-eight, Sing Sing prisoner Number 74699 was paroled to return to Farmingdale a broken man, stripped of his arcane pretenses. But Louis Enricht, when he died shortly afterward, took one secret to his grave. No one has ever proved how he hoodwinked the reporters and Publisher Haskell back in April, 1916.

One explanation, however, seems logical to the point of certainty. It was offered by Thomas Alva Edison's chief engineer, Dr. Miller Reese Hutchinson, who told of a similar "invention" in which water was mixed with acetone, a volatile, inflammable liquid then used in smokeless gunpowder. The scientist duplicated this mixture, took it to the Brooklyn Navy Yard, and ran an engine with it.

"But isn't that a substitute for gasoline after all?" Dr. Hutchinson was asked by a reporter.

"Why, yes," he said, "but you should have seen the cylinders when our experiment was over. The engine was corroded out of commission. You see, the water was merely a vehicle to get the explosive into the cylinders. It was as if a man took the ashes from his furnace and saturated them with oil. They would burn, but then the ashes would be left as before and unless you put in some more oil, you could not get another fire out of them."

If that disposes of Enricht's chemical legerdemain, it does not destroy the fact that he was a talented man with an exceptionally selective mind. Starting out as he did with no scientific education, Louis Enricht learned how to absorb exactly what technical data he would need and to repel all information that would only clutter his mind. The narrowness of this kind of knowledge made it impossible for him to debate the validity of his "formulas" with genuine scientists, but he understood that such discussions would rarely be necessary. Instead, he counted on the public to accept his likely tale as reality. And people did.

The ability to analyze human nature that perceptively is one of the acquired skills that makes a successful scamp successful.

CHAPTER X

"With This Machine, Gentlemen..."

THE HEADLINE was Page One and electrifying: "Air and water harnessed!" The story said:

The scientific world is greatly excited by discovery of a new motive power—power from cold water and air, a vapor more powerful than steam and considerably more economical. The wonderful power of this new creation will supply all the needs of man.

One might think this report concerned the harnessing of the atom, and that it might have appeared in 1945, when revelation of the atomic bomb inspired speculation about the marvelous ways in which atomic energy would serve mankind. The news did concern atomic energy, but that is where similarity ends and an incredible story of scientific swindlery begins.

The dispatch was dated June 11, 1875, and dealt, unwittingly, with a scientific swindle as preposterous as it was gigantic. Behind it was a Philadelphia band leader, circus performer, and carpenter whose scientific ignorance did not bar him from financial success. He took a couple of physics axioms, added a dash of speculation, tailored his pronouncements to the most pressing problems of the day, and milked a fortune from people who knew as much as he did but were willing to believe that he knew more.

The drama began on November 10, 1874, when John Worrell Keely demonstrated his "new motive power" before a group of hard-headed men of common sense. Three hours later, these same men put aside everything they had ever learned about science and sat dumbfounded and worshipful.

Keely's manner was one of solidity and respectability. Tall and powerfully built, he stood coatless in his laboratory on North Twentieth Street in Philadelphia. His dark eyes flickered rapidly and his huge, grimy hands drummed excitedly on his machinery as he talked. The words tumbled out in nervous pace with his movements. He was earnestness itself.

"With this machine, gentlemen," he said, "I can take a twenty-car train from Philadelphia to New York and return. There will be no cinders, no coal, no escaping steam, no dropping coals to set the bridges afire. The device should cost no more than $2,500, perhaps as little as $500."

Murmurs of skepticism arose and Keely shut them off with shortness.

"Gentlemen," he added, "I will draw the power out of as much water as you can hold in your palm. A gallon would propel a steamship from New York to Liverpool and return. But do not take my word, please."

He removed his stern gaze from the observers and

turned to his apparatus. Beside him stood a motor that consisted of a series of hollow metal cylinders arranged like bass drums around an axle. Connected with the motor by a thin platinum wire was another drum-shaped device he called a transmitter, made up of steel plates and tubes. In holes at the base of the transmitter were several tuning forks of various pitches. These forks, the assemblage was shortly to learn, were like none they had ever seen.

Keely drew water from a spigot and poured a pint into one of the motor's cylinders. He secured the petcock and stepped back. He tapped one of the tuning forks and, after a moment, the motor turned.

One of the observers almost babbled, "Why, man, it's incredible! It will revolutionize the world!"

Keely raised his hand. "Wait, gentlemen," he said. "Let this new force really perform."

He attached an inch-thick rope to the motor's axle and secured the other end to a hook suspended from the ceiling. The motor spun and tore the rope apart without changing speed. He attached an iron bar to the shaft and it was twisted double. He made weights rise and fall in a column of water. He attached a belt to the shaft, a chain saw to the belt, and cut thick logs of wood. He geared a hollow copper ball to the shaft and it whirled round and round at six hundred revolutions a minute.

Everyone's eyes darted, looking for a hidden source of power. None could be seen.

Among the audience was a patent lawyer who, after having met Keely earlier, had initiated this demonstration. He was Charles B. Collier, who arose now.

"Mr. Keely," he said, "obviously we could not understand the scientific basis for your discovery, but can you tell us something of how it operates? What makes it work?"

Keely ran bulb-knuckled fingers through his iron-gray sidewhiskers and sat down in a swivel chair, facing away from the men. Then he whirled swiftly. "I can tell you simply this," he said. "Molecular vibration is involved. The atoms and molecules are oscillated by sympathetic equilibrium. All matter consists of atomic triplets and when I apply harmonics there is etheric disintegration. It is that simple and that complex."

The onlookers nodded, as if they understood. Their intoxication was complete.

The next afternoon they gathered in an atmosphere of secrecy in a parlor of the Fifth Avenue Hotel in New York. Attorney Collier told the assembled bankers, merchants, and engineers that they were almost in on the ground floor, but conceded that some New Englanders had already secured territorial rights from Keely for $80,000. They would build Keely motors as quickly as the inventor perfected his discovery. They stood ready with $200,000 more in cash and plans for a $3,000,000 stock company. The rest of the shower of opportunities, Collier explained, would rain on this group.

In five minutes $10,000 had been raised, and a week later, $90,000 more. The Keely Motor Company was incorporated with Keely as president and Collier as treasurer and counsel. Keely moved from drab personal quarters into a pleasurable Oxford Street house.

Immediately after the newspapers announced Keely's "discovery" the following June, the company proceeded to sell $1,000,000 worth of stock—20,000 shares at fifty dollars apiece. They sold feverishly and Keely suddenly acquired a chestnut trotter and carriage, which he grandly paced through Philadelphia's Fairmount Park.

The first discordant note was struck but two weeks later. The well-regarded *Scientific American* flatly referred to Keely's new motive force as "a deception whose chief purpose appears to be the wriggling of money out of silly people."

Keely sighed without commenting and the journal's outrage went largely unnoticed. A month later the public read something infinitely more exciting than criticism. An Ontario man said he had a motor operating that derived power merely from a mixture of nine parts of air and one part coal gas. The gas, the Canadian explained, acted as an explosive. He challenged Keely to an immediate trial of motors.

Keely ignored such carrying-on as unworthy of his scientific dignity, an act that disappointed the curious but inspired their respect. The Canadian's statement also prompted some unbelievers to modify their certainty that what Keely claimed to do couldn't be done. They grudgingly conceded that if two unconnected inventors came up with the same discovery, it could well be a legitimate advance in human knowledge, and a stupendous advance at that.

This reasoning was largely responsible for Keely's success. He had used as the cornerstone of his "theory" the nineteenth-century supposition that a substance called ether permeated all matter. This ether was thought to be the binder that not only held molecules and atoms of molecules together, but wedded the nuclei of atoms themselves. Keely referred to these structures as "atomic triplets." When his peculiar jargon was stripped away his claim was that he had found a way to separate the molecules in such a manner as to release the ether in violent form. This force would multiply and go on to smash the atoms, too, and release their ether in the form of an even more powerful "etheric vapor."

Omitting the ether, this phenomenon was, of course, the heart of what we now know as the chain reaction of atomic energy.

That, at least, is what Keely claimed. The tuning forks, he said, were at the fount of the whole process. Sound was his smashing agent, and the forks were the source of sound waves whose vibrations would be enlarged by his transmitter until they operated his "vibratory engine." He could achieve the same effect by playing a harmonica or a zither to the transmitter, he added. It was all a matter of harmonics.

The editors of the Philadelphia *Bulletin* found this too bulky to swallow and sent a scientifically grounded reporter over for a zither recital. Keely performed and the man came away saying he didn't fully understand what he had seen. "One thing, however, is certain," he wrote. "The power used is cold vapor. It is generated without heat, without light, without chemicals. And it may be stated, and it is stated absolutely, without fear of contradiction, that the force generated from a quart of water is sufficient of itself to propel an ocean steamer."

Sales of Keely motor stocks surged.

Keely himself said little as he continued to spin and whirl devices in his laboratory, but questions piled up. Reporters insisted he explain his secret more fully. But the inventor replied that he could not let anyone in on it or its commercial value to the stockholders would be impaired. He said he owed them a debt—and he certainly did, for his stocks were bulling the market.

"Why don't you apply for a patent?" he was asked.

He assumed a conspiratorial air. "Not until I can secure patents around the world. Soon."

He maintained public interest by continuing his awesome demonstrations and by dropping inspired hints of things to come. Final success, he said, awaited only the finding of a material that could make an engine strong enough to handle the vast power he could create.

But doubts persisted. A year after the first announcement of the great discovery, one newspaper—perhaps in pique over its original splash play of the story—made this heady editorial comment:

The world has great respect for inventive genius, but when a man continually announces for a long period that he has invented a new motor which he is never quite ready to exhibit, the desire to kill him, and thus silence his aggravating claims forever, becomes one of the strongest passions ever developed in the human breast.

Such comment dampened interest in Keely's stock, and its price and volume of sale diminished month by month. By 1878 he had used up his funds and had to face his investors. More than up to the task, though, he burst into their conference at the Fifth Avenue Hotel in New York and announced: "I have abandoned the idea of applying my vaporic power to ordinary engines. I have found that a new engine of a different sort is needed. I am so confident now that I have succeeded that I will stake all I have in the world on results to be accomplished in the next three months."

An hour later Keely had a fresh supply of money to stake. He had persuaded the stockholders not to forsake their golden egg, which would hatch with but a little more warming. One skeptical investor caught Keely by the arm on the way out. "Exactly how does this thing work, Mr. Keely?" he asked. "That's what we want to know."

Keely's face portrayed harassment. "The apparatus will be in use twenty years before it is fully understood," he replied. He darted along the corridor and out into Fifth Avenue.

Two years later, in 1880, he faced the investors once more. His promise of results was now twenty-one months overdue. He demanded that newsmen be barred from the meeting.

"Gentlemen," he said, "I have been able to generate such limitless power that it will now be possible to send a Keely-motored train from here to San Francisco at a mile a minute. A mile a minute, gentlemen! And soon!"

The investors adopted a resolution that proclaimed: "Keely is master of the situation," and handed it to members of the press.

Leading scientists, if not stockholders, became openly derisive. One said he had heard of cold vapor, or fog, but that he really couldn't comprehend a fog engine. Cold vapor, he pointed out, would not expand.

To such talk Keely applied his studied half smile of pity and retorted, "That is true, of course. What the gentleman does not seem to want to understand is that I vibrate the vapor atomically, which expands and energizes it." He went on with his motor spinning and his trotting in Fairmount Park.

A turning point had to come in the inventor's running

joust with money and fame, and in 1881, it did. The Keely Motor Company's treasury held nineteen dollars and forty-eight cents after a thorough milking, and the stockholders' grumblings were becoming ominous. They spoke of deception and misrepresentation, and finally threatened court action.

Keely was untroubled. He enjoyed the situation, for he understood the beguiling point involved. The stockholders were not implying that there was no secret and no new motive power. They were sure there was a secret, and that he had it. They wanted him to share it with someone so it would not be lost if anything should happen to him. One day they firmly refused to grant him further funds unless he confided in at least one man, whom they would select. Keely spent less lavishly and put them off.

He became concerned over the stockholders' attitude, but rescue arrived in the form of a $10,000 check signed by a Philadelphia doctor whose name has never been revealed. The curiousness of the check writer's anonymity was underscored by the fact that at that same time a new benefactor, a well-known woman, entered Keely's drama. She was Mrs. Clara Bloomfield Moore, a Philadelphia poet and etiquette writer, a sort of Emily Post of her day. Mrs. Moore nurtured the pseudonym habit, and her writings regularly appeared under a profusion of names, including those of men.

Mrs. Moore arranged to meet Keely, and instantly became an enthusiastic patron. She had inherited a great deal of money from her late husband and was executrix of his will. Despite the strong objections of her son, Clarence B. Moore, later a highly regarded naturalist, large parts of the inheritance began to pass over to Keely. The suspicion developed that the anonymous "Philadelphia physician" was the many-pseudonymed Mrs. Moore. In any event, Keely was again flush.

The trusting lady was not without some qualms, of course. Once she asked Keely to confide his secret to Thomas Alva Edison, who had just produced an incandescent light bulb. Keely, knowing of Edison's difficulties in perfecting his invention, replied that this would be pointless.

"Edison will never turn out a workable light until he uses my new force as its source of power," he declared. Mrs. Moore thrilled. She felt immersed in the whirlpool of scientific history-in-the-making.

While the lady's entrance pleased Keely, it made his stockholders all the more apprehensive. Worried that the inventor's newly found source of revenue might make him independent of them, they sued to force him to share his secret with their appointee. A court ordered him to do so.

He evidenced no ill feeling as he heard the stockholders wrangle over their choice and finally name a mechanic, William Boekel, to become the repository of the historic secret.

Every morning for three months, Boekel strode into Keely's laboratory. Terrific explosions shook the house all day. Boekel began his inspections in April, 1882, but at the end of July he still was not ready to report. Grumbling erupted again and some stockholders said they hadn't wanted Boekel anyway, that the mechanic had worked for Keely previously, manufacturing parts for his machinery.

In December Boekel finally reported. He said he was completely satisfied with what he had seen and that he understood the principle involved. The following August, Keely told his board of directors his engine would be finished and ready for operation on Labor Day. There would be a Keely train, he said, powered by his atomic energy. It would run from Philadelphia to New York.

The stockholders declared that the inventor's vindication was close at hand. Applications for seats on the Keely train poured in. But Labor Day passed and no Keely train pulled out. The inventor said he was having difficulty controlling the immense power he created. Such enormous force could not be turned loose without adequate checkreins, he warned. It would not be safe. The investors fidgeted, but gave him more money.

Keely's luck was always well-timed, and now he got the ear of Colonel John Hamilton of U. S. Army Ordnance. Hamilton visited his laboratory and was so impressed with a "vaporic gun" Keely showed him that he wrote Secretary of War Robert Lincoln about it. Lincoln sanctioned a demonstration.

One day shortly afterward, Keely arrived at the Sandy Hook Proving Grounds in a special car put at his disposal by the Philadelphia and Reading Railroad. Three hundred persons waited. Captain George Van Reed told them that dynamite was "not worth a continental" beside Keely's Vaporic Gun; he did not mention that he was a Keely investor himself.

As Keely marched up to the gun, a band played "Some Day." No one, however, thought that was a sarcastic appraisal of the inventor's efforts. Patent lawyer Charles Collier held a group of New York stockholders and reporters at bay with the declaration that, "No one but scientific men can understand it. This gun business is simply the reverse of everything hitherto known in science."

At least one reporter agreed. He was from the *Scientific American*, and he took detailed notes throughout the wizardous exhibition that followed.

Keely brought out a small steel tube. In it, he said, was etheric vapor he had made in his laboratory by jarring loose the atoms of the components of plain air. He opened the gun's stopcock, piped etheric vapor into the breech and shut it tight. Then he stepped back, waited five seconds and rapped the gun smartly with a heavy wooden mallet. A cartridge exploded and a bullet shot five hundred yards to a target. After nineteen rounds were fired, a steel bullet was driven through a four-inch log.

The gun was opened and the observers crowded forward to examine the "inter-atomic ether" as it puffed out in a white cloud. It had no taste and no identifiable odor. This same vapor, used in a different way, Keely said, could move tons.

Almost everyone left in high enthusiasm and the next day Keely motor stocks bounced up six points. The unenthusiastic exception was the *Scientific American* reporter, who called the proceedings "another chapter in the history of this timeworn stock-jobbing deception." He said the "atomic ether" was tasteless and odorless because it was nothing but air. Except, he added, that it was compressed air, with which anyone could make a gun fire. The mallet tapping, he said, was unvarnished hocus-pocus worthy of a low grade fortune teller.

But the science writer's voice was lost in the echoes of applause the demonstration earned. Keely, lounging in an initialed dressing gown in the parlor of his residence, told a writer, "My experimenting days are over. I can now produce a projection power thrice greater than gunpowder." He said the ingredients of his Sandy Hook ether had been six drops of water and one pint of air.

"If that force were ever to get out of control," he declared, "and you hit at it with a hatchet, you would break the hatchet, although the implement would hit nothing visible."

The inventor was fairly well left alone over the next three years as he put "the final perfecting touches" to his device. Periodically he told his stockholders that he was almost able to run Philadelphia's factories all day on one morning's charge of inter-atomic ether. Then they issued confident statements, such as one that said, "When this engine is done the long labors of Mr. Keely will be over and the world will know more about the molecular and atomic divisions of matter than ever before."

Through all this the bountiful Mrs. Moore stood by his side, with the cashbox in her excited hands.

Then Keely ran into luck even he couldn't handle. For him, 1888 was a jarring year. Just after New Year's Day, a ghost returned to haunt him. A man named Bennett C. Wilson sued, saying he had hired Keely, in 1863, to varnish furniture for him, and had soon discovered that he had an inventive turn of mind. He had many ideas, and Wilson agreed to furnish him with materials and money in return for a half interest in Keely's inventions. At one point, Wilson charged, Keely had devised a motor that employed a new force, and being in trouble financially, had sold all rights in the device to Wilson.

That machine, Wilson said, was the same one Keely was now selling stock in. It was his. He asked the court to make Keely allow a committee of experts to compare the original plans with the present motor. Keely was ordered to do so. He refused and was brought into court to face a contempt charge.

For a week lawyers wrangled. Representing Keely were Charles Collier and Wayne MacVeagh, who had been United States attorney general seven years earlier under President Garfield. Despite such legal talent, Keely was found guilty.

On a Saturday afternoon in November, 1888, he strode into Common Pleas Court to hear his sentence. He took off a long black coat, stood before the bench, and began to read a lengthy statement. The judge wrote as Keely spoke, and it seemed he was taking notes. But when the boom-voiced inventor finished and the judge read his notes, they turned out to be a commitment to prison until Keely cleared himself of contempt.

The faker sagged. He was quickly led out the back way into Independence Square and taken to Moyamensing Prison.

Cell 150 was nine by fourteen, carpetless, and chilly. After a Sunday breakfast of bread and coffee from the prison wagon, Keely sat on a stool and heard Sunday services through the open door of the prison. A choir and organ rendered "Nearer My God to Thee," and the iron-haired man, now sixty-one, listened intently.

At the prison gates, a sallow youth, who said he was an inventor, asked to see Keely. As he was turned away he shouted that Keely's jailing reminded him of Galileo's imprisonment for advanced thinking in his own day.

Attorney Collier, meanwhile, was in a lather. "This persecution is a criminal conspiracy," he said, "and we will get to the bottom of it. Keely's secret is his own and no power on earth has the right to wring it from him."

Collier and Wayne MacVeagh got the Pennsylvania Supreme Court to fix $1,000 bail until the conviction could be appealed. On Tuesday Keely emerged from his cell and supporters cheered him all the way home.

The following January, when the State Supreme Court reversed his conviction and cleared him, Keely triumphantly dropped more stock into the market and watched it sell briskly. Not all investors were optimistic, however, and one made a well-publicized demonstration of papering his bedroom walls with one hundred shares.

But few remained gloomy for long, because Keely suddenly announced that his etheric vapor had been found suitable for powering an aircraft. The world was waiting eagerly for an airplane, and many thought Keely might have the elusive answer, even though he still couldn't get a patent on his discovery. The narrow-minded Patent Office people, he explained, took the position that "great truths" weren't patentable.

Mrs. Moore, who continued to support Keely financially as the years passed, decided in 1894 that controversy should be ended. She invited a distinguished scientist, Edward A. Scott, to make a thorough investigation of Keely's laboratory. After several visits, Scott advised her to save her money.

"He's an old fraud," the scientist said. He informed the shocked woman that the thin platinum wire that carried Keely's "sound waves" to the motor, where they were vibrated into power, was not a wire at all. It was a cleverly made hollow tube that carried compressed air to do every trick Keely claimed for his new motive force. He had not found the source of the compressed air, Scott said, but was sure it was concealed on the premises.

Mrs. Moore was taken aback, but not convinced. She called on Professor Wentworth Lascelles-Scott of London to make a second investigation. He came over, witnessed the Keely demonstrations, and reported that everything was on the up and up. He even began delivery of a series of lectures before the Franklin Institute in Philadelphia, in which he proposed to explain the Keely phenomenon.

Before he could deliver his second lecture, however, the professor was visited by his predecessor in probing, Edward Scott, who asked if he had inspected the platinum wire. Lascelles-Scott said he had.

"Did you find it to be hollow?"

"No," Lascelles-Scott said. "I took a piece right off a reel on the wall and broke it open. It was wire."

The Philadelphia scientist was shocked. "You mean to say," he asked, "that you didn't inspect the actual wire used on the machine?"

Lascelles-Scott was chagrined. An hour later, he had heard the whole story of Edward Scott's investigation. The next day he left for London without saying good-by to Mrs. Moore.

Mrs. Moore was bewildered, but she did not lose faith, because Keely now said he would prove before the end of the year that he had devised a practical commercial engine. On the strength of this, she asked the wealthy John Jacob Astor to join in capitalizing a new $10,000,000 stock company. Astor, she said, agreed—providing Keely let someone in on his secret.

He refused, but Mrs. Moore was unable to press the point because the inventor had become ill. He was sixty-

eight now, and had a serious kidney ailment. His benefactor stood with him as he made a new announcement.

He had another new device, he said, that would employ
his motive force to drive streetcars. It would be placed in
a small box, he said, and hooked to the front platform of
the cars. Without being connected to their running gear,
it would propel them. He promised an early demonstration.

Fantastically enough, the stockholders then agreed to
issue 400,000 more shares of stock, half the proceeds of
which would go to Keely.

But the end was drawing near. On November 18, 1898,
the old rogue died. This was the event that had frightened
the stockholders for years. They had feared Keely would
take his secret to his grave.

It was to be otherwise, though, and drastically so.

When, four months after Keely's death, Mrs. Moore
died too, her son rented the building on which the inventor's laboratory stood, and arranged for top-flight engineers and scientists to examine it from top to bottom. They
ripped up the flooring and ceiling. Beneath the floor of
Keely's study they found a huge steel sphere, almost buried
in dirt and rubbish and held down by heavy beams. At its
top was an iron pipe which, fifteen feet away, connected
with a thin platinum tube of the kind found leading to
Keely's motor. The tube was traced through holes in the
flooring and up through orifices in the heavy legs of the
"transmitter."

The investigators had discovered the source of Keely's
"new motive power." It was compressed air from the
sunken sphere. For his Sandy Hook "vapor gun" demonstration, they now realized, he had simply filled a steel

tube with compressed air from the sphere and piped it into the gun.

Compressed air was Keely's only true secret.

"He was an unadulterated rascal," said Mrs. Moore's son. But at a memorial meeting arranged by faithful followers, the fervor still ran like sap in the spring. "We are on the verge of a much higher stage of society than many dream of," said a mournful orator, "and John Worrell Keely has been one of the greatest pioneers."

Seven years later, in 1905, Albert Einstein published the first of his theories of relativity, which led to the genuine harnessing of atomic energy and proved the non-existence of any such substance as "inter-atomic ether." Unlike Keely, however, Einstein didn't need compressed air to make his point.

CHAPTER XI

A Gaggle of Sharpshooters

THE TROUBLE with this gallery of rascals is the trouble with life: there is never room enough for everything. And so, just as some swindlers have evaded being brought to book, some have so far evaded this tour of rascality. The purpose of the following omnibus excursion, therefore, is to bring these bounders to *this* book, if to no other.

Their escapades illustrate the creative instinct in dedicated swindlers. They all operated with inventiveness that distinguishes them from garden-variety criminals, and they show that it is much easier to see through a swindle after its conclusion than during its unfolding. The capacity to be taken in—credulity—is often manufactured by artful swindlers as much as it is offered by victims.

The first of these episodes is a geographical exception; it did not take place in the United States but it is included nonetheless because American know-how has not yet contributed as remarkable a feat. Perhaps it will inspire one.

When Louis de Rougemont arrived in London around the turn of the century, after spending thirty years as a cannibal chieftain, and reported that his wife had eaten his baby, skepticism was only to be expected. But lanky, sun-baked de Rougemont presented himself to the editors of a British periodical and offered to recount his experiences for their readers. The editors, astonished and dubious, sub-mitted the man and his works to leading anthropologists, geographers, and world travelers. These men questioned de Rougemont closely, checked his report against personal and documentary knowledge, and then assured the editors they could publish the memoirs without hesitation. The result was a smashing splash of morbidity.

De Rougemont explained that he had been aboard a sailing vessel in the late 1860's when a storm off New Guinea wrecked the boat and beached him on a tiny, un-inhabited island, where he soon realized he was the sole survivor. Being an adaptable type, he decided to make the most and best of his predicament, and started by establish-ing an unusual riding sport.

"I waded out to where the turtles were," he said, "and on catching a six-hundred-pounder, sat on his back. Away the startled creature swam a foot or so below the surface. When he dived deeper I simply sat back on the shell and he had to come up." Steering the turtle was no more diffi-cult. To turn left, de Rougemont stuck a toe in the turtle's right eye and to go right, vice versa. A toe in both eyes acted as a brake.

Amusing himself in this manner and subsisting appetiz-ingly enough on plentiful vegetation and small animals, the nineteenth century Robinson Crusoe was joined one day by a family of four unclothed, friendly South Sea Islanders whose bark had been overturned and lost in a gale. The woman's name was Yamba and although her nude body embarrassed the somewhat prissy de Rougemont, his good manners triumphed and he shed his clothes too. Soon he was making his conversational way through his companions' language.

Since the tiny island was limited in the sustenance it could provide, the involuntary adventurer convinced his friends they should try to reach the Australian mainland. They built a crude craft and set out, but were blown by a strong wind to Yamba's native island. The area seemed to have been full of storms, gales, and strong winds.

In any event, Yamba's countrymen were gracious; they invited de Rougemont to live with them and offered to find him a bride. He and Yamba were by then so mutually attracted, though, that her husband obligingly stepped aside and the pair were joined in balmy matrimony.

So devoted was Yamba that many modern husbands would worship her. When de Rougemont asked for salt one day, she tramped miles to find some sprigs of salt herbs. Daily she brought him delectable kangaroo meat and a variety of fish, and just as daily his life became more idyllic. Unfortunately, however, a day came when he was shocked to learn that his new countrymen were preparing to gorge themselves on some other countrymen who had just died.

The women scraped trenches and placed the bodies in them. Then the trenches were filled with stones and sand. On top, a fire burned fiercely for two hours. "When the ovens were opened," de Rougemont said, "I looked in and saw the bodies were very burnt. The skin was cracked and liquid fat was issuing forth. At the moment the roasted carcasses were taken out the whole tribe fell on them and tore them limb from limb. I saw mothers with a leg or an arm surrounded by children crying for their portion of the toothsome dainty."

Despite his initial horror, de Rougemont's infinite adaptability prevailed and he accepted the custom, although he continued ordering kangaroo and fish for himself. It was shortly after this traumatic episode that he became chief of the tribe by, ironically, running away from an attacking alligator. By chance he led the beast directly to Yamba, who thrust a strong bough down its throat and killed it; the islanders mistook his flight for a resourceful bit of strategy.

The apex of de Rougemont's epic saga came when he was stricken with malaria and was nursed through his delirium by Yamba, who was then in an advanced state of pregnancy. Upon his recovery he realized that she was no longer pregnant, and asked to see his baby.

"Yamba told me she had eaten it," he related. "I asked her why."

"I could not have nursed both of you," she said, "so I did what I considered best." For a good while Yamba dangled a small bark parcel from her neck; it contained some of the infant's bones, which she was preserving in memoriam.

After a number of equally colossal adventures, de Rougemont managed to leave the island and make his way to London and fame. The first article of his odyssey caused a tremendous stir, of course, and soon the elderly, tropics-burned man was lecturing before women's tea clubs and even the British Association for the Advancement of Science. His writings were translated into several languages and he basked in the warmth of attention.

But as all bubbles burst, so too did this one. A news-

paper published by incurable cynics probed the story and
one day printed a devastating exposé. The man's name
wasn't de Rougemont, it was Grin. He wasn't a Briton-
turned-cannibal-chief, he was a bored Swiss butler-turned-
romantic. He hadn't spent years in the South Seas but in
the library of the British Museum!

As dramatically as he had appeared, de Rougemont-
Grin vanished. He had swindled his fellow men out of a
small amount of money and a fleeting brush with fame,
but who can say he did not give good value in exchange?
Think how many humdrum lives he brightened, how
many chill winter evenings were warmed by the reading
of his fantasy. De Rougemont-Grin exemplified the artistic
element in swindling, an element not found in the man
apprehended for crude armed robbery.

The American who most closely matched de Rougemont-Grin in the art of posing was Frederick Peters, a
mild nobody who became almost everybody who was
anybody. Peters was a confirmed bad check passer who
elevated a mundane calling by using inspired techniques.
In contrast with many rascals, he was never greedy—an
FBI report called him "the most extraordinarily lenient
swindler on record." But he was always enterprising.

Peters opened a lifetime career of impersonation at the
age of nineteen by enlisting in the Navy under one name
after he had deserted under another. He was discovered
and discharged but his little joke intrigued him. Between
1906, when he first became somebody else, and 1931, when
he completed a seven-year term in a Federal penitentiary
for forgery, he made many mistakes but also advanced the
state of his art. He learned that nothing impresses so much

as an impressive name. Moreover, if it is not your own name its assets may be enjoyed and the liabilities left to its original owner.

Arriving in Chicago at the height of the Depression, Peters decided that straightaway impersonation was a gambit that needed modification. So he added a wrinkle; he impersonated by association. Instead of calling himself Paul Du Pont, he became Paul Du Pont, Jr.; not Clement Studebaker, but Clement Studebaker III. In his time, he was also known as Theodore Roosevelt II.

His dress was appropriately neat and expensive and his taste refined. He visited exclusive shops and ordered matched luggage, fine paintings, pedigreed puppies, and costly bric-a-brac. And he always paid with a check written for a figure higher than the purchase. He even married under another name and swindled the preacher out of the difference between his fee and the amount of a large check.

Peters was so proud of his method that he is known to have modified it only once, when he wired his parents a report of his own death and asked for money to have his body shipped home. He signed the telegram with a name chosen at random from the Chicago telephone directory, then picked up the money and departed for Florida, where he fleeced several land-boomers who tried to fleece *him* with acreage on the miraculously ever-expanding Florida ocean front.

He didn't leave in time and was caught, tried, and convicted, but the experience was not a total loss. While editing the prison magazine, he practiced his art of persuasion by writing to prominent authors and inducing them to contribute articles without payment. (As any writer

knows, this a formidable feat.) The warden was so taken
with the man that he assigned him to chauffeur his wife
on shopping trips.

After his release, Peters renewed his impersonations until
he was wanted in a dozen states under as many names. One
of his headier escapades took place on Park Avenue in
New York, where he browsed through an art gallery
after handing a clerk an engraved calling card that read
"Franklin Delano Roosevelt III, Hyde Park, New York."
The clerk couldn't readily place the III but the thrill of
serving anyone in that illustrious family was enough to
make questions stillborn. Peters selected a half-dozen rend-
erings of sailing ships—F. D.R. I was known to be fond of
the sea—had them them sent out, and wrote his customary
oversized check with a flourishing signature. When the
paintings arrived at Hyde Park the investigation that followed placed Peters on the FBI's Most Wanted list.

It was not until 1952 that the imaginative poser was
tracked down, and then only after he had passed the war
years by impersonating a host of minor government officials in search of materials, priorities, and other flotsam of
wartime. An FBI man, who discovered him reading a philosophy book in a Washington hotel lobby, refused to
believe he was a man named Carpenter who wanted the
State Department to sponsor a musical pageant in Venezuela. The jury didn't believe him either, and Peters got
three to nine years, which was a boon to people with glittering family names.

As Frederick Peters confined his role-playing to men of
means, Harold Rain confined his to men of medicine. For
seven very recent years he proved that credulity consists

of little more than not being suspicious of apparent normality.

What formal medical education he had, Harold Rain gathered by dropping into classes at the University of Illinois College of Medicine, in Chicago. He was not a registered student, but since educational institutions do not expect their walls to be scaled by irregular hungerers for knowledge, he attracted no suspicion.

Being a young veteran of World War II, pleasant bespectacled Rain applied for a position with the Veterans administration. His claims to a medical degree and license were not investigated because of hurry and confusion and he was retained to admit patients to a veterans' hospital near Chicago. There he remained for almost six months, or until he was told that an FBI man wanted to see him. He left, not knowing the agent was interested in one of his patients, not in the patient's doctor.

Rain then became Dr. Samuel Pike Hall, a California physician whose name he found in a medical directory, and posed as industrial doctor, hospital resident, and obstetrician and gynecologist throughout the Midwest. In Texas, he held sick call for civilians at the Army's Fort Sam Houston. He rarely remained in a post more than a year, usually exciting suspicion only when he left without notice because of unpleasantnesses with local finance companies.

During his travels, Rain performed a huge number of operations ranging from hysterectomies to surgery for hernias. He was not a bad surgeon—neither brilliant nor dismal. One of the rare times he came close to losing a patient was when he overlooked a postoperative compli-

cation; fortunately, another doctor recognized the condition in time.

In the course of his unlettered career, Rain's salary sometimes reached $1,000 a month, but he had an insatiable
appetite for clothes and cars. Part of his debt to San
Antonio, Texas, consisted of $5,600 in department store
bills. Elsewhere, finance companies and banks held his
notes for automobile and personal loans.

In 1953, after several notices of his imposture had
appeared in the *Journal of the American Medical Associ-
tion,* Rain decided to retire from practice. Romantic to
the end, he turned himself in to *The Saturday Evening
Post,* whose editors notified the authorities. Rain got off
with three years, but the *Post* was so intrigued with the
story that it later published a detailed saga of his life. As a
result of that publicity, Harold Rain will probably practice forbearance rather than medicine in the future.

American magazines and newspapers have played host
to a good number of swindles, most of them harmless,
some brilliantly entertaining. In 1941, for example, a bored
stockbroker fed scores of a nonexistent team to the New
York *Times* for most of a football season. But the meatiest
swindle of many years was paid for by the staid *Atlantic
Monthly* in 1928. It was then, three score and seven years
after Abraham Lincoln had entered the White House, that
a woman set forth to cash in on alleged love letters to and
from Ann Rutledge.

The years in which the letters were supposedly written
was 1834, when Lincoln was twenty-five. Ann, twenty-
one, was the talk of New Salem, Illinois, because her
fiancé had jilted her. Although Lincoln paid much atten-

tion to Ann before her death in 1835, no student of the man's life—and that includes Carl Sandburg—had been able to supply a record of correspondence between them.

That gap was filled in 1928 when a California woman sent such correspondence to Ellery Sedgwick, editor of the *Atlantic Monthly*. From its safe perch of conservatism, the magazine minced no words in the title it gave the series: "Lincoln the Lover." Sedgwick announced that "the love story of Lincoln and Ann can be fully told for the first time."

"My beloved Abe," one letter began. "My hart runs over with hapynes when I think yore name. . . . I dream of yore words every nite and long for you by day. I must git super now. All my heart is ever thine. Ann."

Lincoln was less demonstrative, but he did allow himself to reply to "My Beloved Ann," and to state his belief that "with you, my beloved, all things are possible." Ann asked Abe to "think of me as I think of you, for I am thine forever and ever," and Lincoln rejoined, "My Dearly Valued Ann. My fervent love is with you."

At least the *Atlantic Monthly* said he did. No sooner did the magazine reach subscribers than questions arose. After some weeks of fairly warm debate with devotees of Lincoln's life, Editor Sedgwick went to California and conferred with the woman who had supplied the letters. When he returned to the East, he announced that the series would be discontinued. But magazines go to press some time before their issue dates, and the *Atlantic* had two more installments of "Lincoln the Lover" in type. With the last installment it published an article that began: "No amateur should be ashamed of occasionally buying a forgery . . ."

About a year before the resurrection of Lincoln's romance, several leading newspapers carried fascinating dispatches from Detroit.

> Colonel Charles A. Lindbergh [one story said], today tested a new type of motor which, it is predicted, will revolutionize power for airplanes and possibly automobiles.
>
> The motor is said to employ electromagnetism in connection with the rotary motion of the earth. It uses no fuel . . . Late today it was taken to an experimental hangar, where the transatlantic flier aided in the tryout.

Then the designer of the tri-motor Ford airplane reported that he, too, had seen a "very impressive demonstration." He understood that the motor drew energy "directly from electrical currents which exist constantly in the air or in the ground."

The inventor of this sensation, a personable twenty-nine-year-old, had a remarkable story to tell. He explained that several years ago he had had a dream in which he saw a motor running on "earth currents," and that recently his four-year-old son had complained because he couldn't get his model airplane to fly. "I remembered the vision," the inventor said, "and I built the fuel-less motor. I put it into the airplane, turned the switch on, and the propeller turned. I just hook it up to the earth's magnetic current and watch it go!"

Follow-up newspaper stories reported that "capitalists have about completed arrangements to purchase the invention, or to control its production. Pilots and mechanics believe it to be the greatest invention of the age . . ."

A professor at the Graduate School of Aeronautics at New York University was skeptical. "The laws of physics are pretty rigid," he said, "and there is no way of getting something for nothing." But this demurrer was lost in an Army officer's announcement that a second model of the motor had been developed with "enough power to kill a man." The Army man conceded that "the whole thing is so mysterious and startling that it has the appearance of being a fake," but added, "I am sure there is nothing phony about it."

The officer was contradicted by an angry Pittsburgh physicist, who reported that he had found tiny batteries concealed in the motor (and that two Pittsburgh industrialists had given the young man $25,000 for an interest in the device). The inventor replied that the batteries were powerless and had been installed only to throw patent jumpers off the track.

A week later the mystery was climaxed by a front page story in the New York *Herald Tribune* revealing that the inventor was in Emergency Hospital, Washington, D. C., recovering from temporary paralysis of his arms and legs. The attending doctor said the young man had been careless with his motor and received an electric shock of two thousand volts.

With his discharge from the hospital the inventor of the age disappeared, taking with him the secret of his fuel-less motor. No further word was heard from backers or other interested parties, and to this day no other inventor has succeeded in harnessing the vast power of the magnetic universe.

Revolutionary-sounding gadgets have had prolonged runs in the annals of dramatic rascality, but their producers have by no means all been frauds; sometimes these devices were products of brilliant minds debilitated by age. That

was the case with Nikola Tesla, who had introduced the
concept of alternating electrical current that made possible transmission of electric power from Niagara Falls.
Tesla delighted in tearing away the veil that surrounded
so many physical forces; it has been said that there is
hardly a modern invention whose fundamentals he didn't
pioneer. Unfortunately, though, his balance went awry
and when he was almost eighty, he slipped into a field that
had been thoroughly mined by crackpots and rascals. He
claimed he had invented an invisible "death ray."

Methods of "broadcasting death by wireless" cropped
up in the news from the time of World War I through
the mid-1930's. First it was the Germans who claimed they
were knocking French planes out of the air with "death
rays." Then an Englishman picked up $100,000 for his
ray, which he demonstrated by exterminating rats at sixty
feet; he sold the British Admiralty the idea of installing
the device in ships. Not to be outdone, a Russian claimed
a similar discovery, and in 1923, just before his exile, Leon
Trotzky investigated it. So it went without tangible results
until 1934, when Nikola Tesla called a press conference
in New York. He was seventy-eight then, and causing
consternation among hotel managers by harboring pigeons
in his rooms.

Tesla said he had devised an invisible ray capable of
shooting 10,000 planes from the air at a distance of 250
miles; an army of 1,000,000 could be struck dead instantly,
he declared. He rambled endlessly and somewhat para-
noically about all the people who were trying to steal and
stifle his invention and, charitably, few newspapers or
periodicals published his claims. He died in 1943, a vacant,

tragic figure whose strongest interest was in feeding the pigeons near the New York Public Library.

If it seems so obvious that fuel-less motors and death rays are frauds, the obviousness results partly from hindsight. Artistic swindlers usually time their discoveries to coincide with a compelling need for what they are offering and thus manufacture credibility, which is too often confused with credulity. Those who feel this is too much an apology for the easily duped, or too generous to the swindler, may test their own credulity quotient by separating the scientific from the silly among the following propositions:

1. An automatic typewriter has been devised that operates by changes in voice pitch.

2. A piano plays music by selecting keys from the frequencies of a phonograph record.

3. Printing can be accomplished without presses by discharging smoke onto paper; the smoke contains electrically charged particles which form words or illustrations.

4. A mechanical invention can exert a pressure of 3,000,000 pounds per square inch, a force normally equaled only in the depths of the earth's core; the force is great enough to compress the space between molecules and reduce an object's mass by ten percent.

5. A machine has been devised that responds not only to pre-set signals, but can read handwritten numbers and words and act on them; it is powered by flashlight batteries.

6. Scientists are seriously considering the possibility of a machine to reduce normal sleep requirements by four-fifths; the theory is to produce extremely short waves that destroy fatigue toxins in the body.

7. A chemist has discovered a liquid that, placed between two metal surfaces, locks them together; a drop will hold bolt

threads so securely that no vibration can shake them loose, yet the bolt can be loosened with common tools.

It would be intriguing to know how many people would invest in the propositions set out under Numbers 3, 4, 5, 6 and 7. They might make some money, for only the voice-driven typewriter and the phonograph-actuated piano are fakes; they were sold for investment purposes by a swindler who operated on the premise that "deep down in all of us there is a fundamental impulse to take a reasonable chance."

But when we take a reasonable chance on what later events prove to be a piece of flummery, we are accused of having been credulous and gullible. Were we?

It would seem that whatever credulity really is, it is at least here to stay—a natural pitfall among our stumbling efforts to distinguish reality from fantasy.

Perhaps a certain amount of credulity is desirable—even essential—in our lives. In December, 1903, die-hard realists scoffed at reports that the Wright brothers had put a plane into the air. (Would you have bought stock in *that* enterprise ten years before Kitty Hawk?) And today we must revise our notions of reality in order to believe that man can place a new planet into nature's solar system. (What would we have said of *that* proposition five years ago?)

And so, as yesterday's rogues pass from memory, we will have to prepare for new schemes, new ideas, new devices, new discoveries, new claims, and we will have to continue trying to distinguish the honest man from the scandalous scamp. Both will be seeking our most valuable asset, which some call credulity and others call faith.

Bibliography

IN INTEGRATING the foregoing gallery of rascals with the times in which they operated, I have relied on newspapers, periodicals, personal interviews, and books dealing with the American scene of the past century.

The full story of Richard Whitney's high-altitude downfall has never been told in book or magazine. In addition to newspaper accounts and personal interviews, I relied heavily on three volumes, *U. S. A. Before the Securities and Exchange Commission in the Matter of Richard Whitney, et al.* (Government Printing Office, 1938). If the title is forbidding, the contents are not; they portray the Wall Street forces that made Whitney's adventures possible. Ferdinand Lundberg also does this very provocatively in *America's 60 Families* (Citadel Press, 1937). Frederick Lewis Allen sets the social stage in *Only Yesterday* (Harper & Bros., 1931), and in *The Great Pierpont Morgan* (Harper & Bros., 1949). John K. Galbraith admirably explains the stock market in *The Great Crash, 1929* (Houghton Mifflin Co., 1955).

Kansas' frenetic politics during the heyday of John R. "Goat-Gland" Brinkley can be entertainingly studied in a candid book, *Rascals In Democracy* (Richard R. Smith, 1940), by an irreverent political observer, W. G. Clugston.

The life and thieving times of "Boss" Tweed can be further explored in Croswell Bowen's excellent *The Elegant Oakey* (Oxford University Press, 1956), in chapters of Meyer Berger's *The Story of The New York Times* (Simon and Schuster, 1951), and in *Boss Tweed* (Boni & Liveright, 1927), by Denis Tilden Lynch. But for a definitive exposition on Tammany Hall from its inception through the nineteenth century, there is Gustavus Myers' indispensable *The History of Tammany Hall* (published by the author, 1901).

As for the gadget-men, the "revolutionary-invention" fakers, and the dilemma of separating genius from crackpot, Gerald W. Johnson brings insight to nonconformism in *The Lunatic Fringe* (J. B. Lippincott Co., 1957), and Charles Fort will leave you gasping in his idol-busting *Wild Talents* (Kendall, 1932). An excellent scientific book is *Fads and Fallacies in the Name of Science* (Dover Publications, 1957), by Martin Gardner, who blends authority with literary skill.

To satisfy a desire for more accounts of straight rascality, there are many books, some good, some superb. These include *True Tales from the Annals of Crime and Rascality* (Random House, 1957), by St. Clair McKelway; Alexander Klein's *Grand Deception* (J. B. Lippincott Co., 1955), and *The Double Dealers* (J. B. Lippincott Co., 1958); Murray Teigh Bloom's *Money of Their Own* (Charles Scribner's Sons, 1957), and Curtiss D. Mac-Dougall's noted *Hoaxes* (Macmillan, 1940)—a fascinating, comprehensive bible of ruses, pranks, hoaxes, and swindles.